The Inconstant by George Farquhar

A COMEDY, IN FIVE ACTS; AS PERFORMED AT THE THEATRE ROYAL, DRURY LANE.

George Farquhar was born in Derry, Ireland in 1677, one of seven children.

Farquhar was educated at Foyle College and later, aged 17, he entered Trinity College, Dublin. He departed after only two years, accounts vary as to why, and he took to acting on the Dublin stage.

As an actor he seems to have had no real talent. A terrible accident, when he failed to distinguish between a tipped foil and a deadly rapier, and seriously wounded a fellow actor, resolved Farquhar to give up acting for good.

His first play, Love and a Bottle, was well received at London's Drury Lane Theatre in 1699 and was admired "for its sprightly Dialogue and busy Scenes."

With the play a success Farquhar settled his talents on a career as a playwright. He had a second play open that same year; The Constant Couple. Again, it was warmly received on debuting at Drury Lane and proved a great success. However, another interest and opportunity now unfolded into his life. He received a commission in the regiment of the Earl of Orrery. His time now became divided between the duties of a successful new playwright and the vocations of soldier.

In 1701 Farquhar wrote and debuted a sequel to the Constant Couple, called and based on its main character; Sir Harry Wildair. The following year was to be prolific for the young playwright. He penned both The Inconstant or, The Way To Win and The Twin-Rivals as well as publishing Love and Business, a collection that included letters, verse, and A Discourse Upon Comedy.

His work for the army, recruiting soldiers to fight in the War of the Spanish Succession, occupied much of his time for the next three years, and he was to write little except The Stage Coach, in 1774.

Farquhar was able, however, to draw upon these years of recruiting experience for his next comedy, The Recruiting Officer in 1706. Early in 1707, Farquhar wrote what was to be his masterpiece: The Beaux Stratagem.

In these last two plays his real contribution to the English drama is all the more apparent. He introduced a verbal vigour and sparring, as well as a love of character that are more usually associated with Elizabethan dramatists and laid much of the foundations for Sheridan and Congreve to build upon.

George Farquhar, aged only 40, died on April 29th, 1707, almost two months after the debut of his greatest work. He was buried in the Church of St. Martin in the Fields, London, on May 3rd, 1707.

Index of Contents

REMARKS by Mrs Elizabeth Inchbald

This comedy, by a favourite writer, had a reception, on the first night of its appearance, far inferior to that of his other productions. It was, with difficulty, saved from condemnation; and the author, in his preface, has boldly charged some secret enemies with having attempted its destruction.

Dramatic authors have fewer enemies at the present period, or they have more humility, than formerly. For now, when their works are hissed from the stage, they acknowledge they have had a fair trial, and deserve their fate. Wherefore should an author seek for remote causes, to account for his failures, when to himself alone, he is certain ever to impute all his success?

Neither the wit, humour, nor the imitation of nature, in this play, are of that forcible kind, with which the audience had been usually delighted by Farquhar; and, that the moral gave a degree of superiority to this drama, was, in those days, of little consequence: the theatre was ordained, it was thought, for mere pleasure, nor did any one wish it should degenerate into instruction.

It may be consolatory to the disappointed authors of the present day, to find, how the celebrated author of this comedy was incommoded with theatrical crosses. He was highly offended, that his play was not admired; still more angry, that there was an empty house, on his sixth night, and more angry still, that the Opera House, for the benefit of a French dancer, was, about this time, filled even to the annoyance of the crowded company. The following are his own words on the occasion:

"It is the prettiest way in the world of despising the French king, to let him see that we can afford money to bribe his dancers, when he, poor man, has exhausted all his stock, in buying some pitiful towns and principalities. What can be a greater compliment to our generous nation, than to have the lady on her re-tour to Paris, boast of her splendid entertainment in England: of the complaisance, liberty, and good nature of a people, who thronged her house so full, that she had not room to stick a pin; and left a poor fellow, who had the misfortune of being one of themselves, without one farthing, for half a year's pains he had taken for their entertainment."

This complaint is curious, on account of the talents of the man who makes it; and, for the same cause, highly reprehensible. If Farquhar, thought himself superior to the French dancer, why did he honour her by a comparison? and, if he wanted bread, why did he not suffer in silence, rather than insinuate, he should like to receive it, through the medium of a benefit?

A hundred years of refinement (the exact time since this author wrote) may have weakened the force of the dramatic pen; but it has, happily, elevated authors above the servile spirit of dedications, or the meaner practice, of taking public benefits.

As the moral of this comedy has been mentioned as one of its highest recommendations, it must be added—that, herein, the author did not invent, but merely adopt, as his own, an occurrence which took place in Paris, about that period, just as he has represented it in his last act. The Chevalier de Chastillon was the man who is personated by young Mirabel, in this extraordinary event; and the Chevalier's friend, his betrothed wife, and his beautiful courtesan, are all exactly described in the characters of Duretete, Oriana, and Lamorce.

Having justly abridged Farquhar of the honour of inventing a moral, it may be equally just, to make a slight apology for his chagrin at the slender receipts of his sixth night.—He once possessed the income, which arose from a captain's commission in the army; and having prudently conceived that this little revenue would not maintain a wife, he had resolved to live single, unless chance should bestow on him a woman of fortune. His person and address were so extremely alluring, that a woman of family, but of no fortune, conceiving the passion she felt for him to be love, pretended she possessed wealth, and deceived him into a marriage, which plunged them both into the utmost poverty.

This admirable dramatist seems to have been born for a dupe. In his matrimonial distress, he applied to a nobleman, who had professed a friendship for him, and besought his advice how to surmount his difficulties: The counsel given, was—"Sell your commission, for present support, and, before the money for its sale is expended, I will procure you another." Farquhar complied—and his patron broke his word.

DRAMATIS PERSONÆ

OLD MIRABEL	Mr. Dowton.
YOUNG MIRABEL	Mr. C. Kemble.
CAPTAIN DURETETE	Mr. Bannister.
DUGARD	Mr. Holland.
PETIT	Mr. De Camp.
BRAVOES	Messrs. Maddocks, Webb, Evans and Sparks.

ORIANA   Mrs. Young.
BISARRE   Mrs. Jordan.
LAMORCE   Miss Tidswell.

THE INCONSTANT

ACT THE FIRST

SCENE I.—The Street

Enter **DUGARD**, and his Man, **PETIT**, in Riding Habits.

DUGARD
Sirrah, what's o'clock?

PETIT
Turned of eleven, sir.

DUGARD
No more! We have rid a swinging pace from Nemours, since two this morning! Petit, run to Rousseau's, and bespeak a dinner, at a Lewis d'or a head, to be ready by one.

PETIT
How many will there be of you, sir?

DUGARD
Let me see—Mirabel one, Duretete two, myself three—

PETIT
And I four.

DUGARD
How now, sir? at your old travelling familiarity! When abroad, you had some freedom, for want of better company, but among my friends, at Paris, pray remember your distance—Begone, sir!

[Exit **PETIT**.]

This fellow's wit was necessary abroad, but he's too cunning for a domestic; I must dispose of him some way else.—Who's here? Old Mirabel, and my sister!—my dearest sister!

Enter **OLD MIRABEL** and **ORIANA**.

ORIANA
My Brother! Welcome!

DUGARD

Monsieur Mirabel! I'm heartily glad to see you.

OLD MIRABEL

Honest Mr. Dugard, by the blood of the Mirabels, I'm your most humble servant!

DUGARD

Why, sir, you've cast your skin, sure; you're brisk and gay—lusty health about you—no sign of age, but your silver hairs.

OLD MIRABEL

Silver hairs! Then they are quicksilver hairs, sir. Whilst I have golden pockets, let my hairs be silver, an' they will. Adsbud, sir, I can dance, and sing, and drink, and—no, I can't wench. But Mr. Dugard, no news of my son Bob in all your travels?

DUGARD

Your son's come home, sir.

OLD MIRABEL

Come home! Bob come home! By the blood of the Mirabels, Mr. Dugard, what say you?

ORIANA

Mr. Mirabel returned, sir?

DUGARD

He's certainly come, and you may see him within this hour or two.

OLD MIRABEL

Swear it, Mr. Dugard, presently swear it.

DUGARD

Sir, he came to town with me this morning; I left him at the Banieurs, being a little disordered after riding, and I shall see him again presently.

OLD MIRABEL

What! and he was ashamed to ask a blessing with his boots on! A nice dog! Well, and how fares the young rogue, ha?

DUGARD

A fine gentleman, sir; he'll be his own messenger.

OLD MIRABEL

A fine gentleman! But is the rogue like me still?

DUGARD

Why, yes, sir; he's very like his mother, and as like you, as most modern sons are to their fathers.

OLD MIRABEL

Why, sir, don't you think that I begat him?

DUGARD

Why, yes, sir; you married his mother, and he inherits your estate. He's very like you, upon my word.

ORIANA

And pray, brother, what's become of his honest companion, Duretete?

DUGARD

Who, the captain? The very same, he went abroad; he's the only Frenchman I ever knew, that could not change. Your son, Mr. Mirabel, is more obliged to nature for that fellow's composition, than for his own: for he's more happy in Duretete's folly than his own wit. In short, they are as inseparable as finger and thumb; but the first instance in the world, I believe, of opposition in friendship.

OLD MIRABEL

Very well: will he be home, to dinner, think ye?

DUGARD

Sir, he has ordered me to bespeak a dinner for us at Rousseau's, at a Lewis d'or a head.

OLD MIRABEL

A Lewis d'or a head! Well said, Bob; by the blood of the Mirabels, Bob's improved! But, Mr. Dugard, was it so civil of Bob, to visit Monsieur Rousseau, before his own natural father, eh? Harkye, Oriana, what think you now, of a fellow that can eat and drink ye a whole Lewis d'or at a sitting? He must be as strong as Hercules; life and spirit in abundance. Before Gad, I don't wonder at these men of quality, that their own wives can't serve them! A Lewis d'or a head! 'tis enough to stock the whole nation with bastards, 'tis, 'faith! Mr. Dugard, I leave you with your sister.

[Exit.

DUGARD

Well, sister, I need not ask you how you do, your looks resolve me; fair, tall, well-shaped; you're almost grown out of my remembrance.

ORIANA

Why, truly, brother, I look pretty well, thank nature, and my toilet; I eat three meals a day, am very merry when up, and sleep soundly when I'm down.

DUGARD

But, sister, you remember that upon my going abroad, you would chuse this old gentleman for your guardian; he's no more related to our family, than Prester John, and I have no reason to think you mistrusted my management of your fortune. Therefore, pray be so kind as to tell me, without reservation, the true cause of making such a choice.

ORIANA

Lookye, brother, you were going a rambling, and 'twas proper, lest I should go a rambling too, that somebody should take care of me. Old Monsieur Mirabel is an honest gentleman, was our father's friend, and has a young lady in his house, whose company I like, and who has chosen him for her guardian as well as I.

DUGARD
Who, Mademoiselle Bisarre?

ORIANA
The same; we live merrily together, without scandal or reproach; we make much of the old gentleman between us, and he takes care of us; all the week we dance and sing, and upon Sundays, go first to church, and then to the play.—Now, brother, besides these motives for chusing this gentleman for my guardian, perhaps I had some private reasons.

DUGARD
Not so private as you imagine, sister; your love to young Mirabel's no secret, I can assure you, but so public, that all your friends are ashamed on't.

ORIANA
O' my word, then, my friends are very bashful; though I'm afraid, sir, that those people are not ashamed enough at their own crimes, who have so many blushes to spare for the faults of their neighbours.

DUGARD
Ay, but, sister, the people say—

ORIANA
Pshaw! hang the people! they'll talk treason, and profane their Maker; must we, therefore infer, that our king is a tyrant, and religion a cheat? Lookye, brother, their court of inquiry is a tavern, and their informer, claret: They think as they drink, and swallow reputations like loches; a lady's health goes briskly round with the glass, but her honour is lost in the toast.

DUGARD
Ay, but sister, there is still something—

ORIANA
If there be something, brother, 'tis none of the people's something: Marriage is my thing, and I'll stick to't.

DUGARD
Marriage! young Mirabel marry! he'll build churches sooner. Take heed, sister, though your honour stood proof to his home-bred assaults, you must keep a stricter guard for the future: He has now got the foreign air, and the Italian softness; his wit's improved by converse, his behaviour finished by observation, and his assurances confirmed by success. Sister, I can assure you, he has made his conquests; and 'tis a plague upon your sex, to be the soonest deceived, by those very men that you know have been false to others.—But then, sister, he's as fickle—

ORIANA
For God's sake, brother, tell me no more of his faults, for, if you do, I shall run mad for him: Say no more, sir; let me but get him into the bands of matrimony, I'll spoil his wandering, I warrant him; I'll do his business that way, never fear.

DUGARD

Well, sister, I won't pretend to understand the engagements between you and your lover; I expect when you have need of my counsel or assistance, you will let me know more of your affairs. Mirabel is a gentleman, and as far as my honour and interest can reach, you may command me, to the furtherance of your happiness: In the mean time, sister, I have a great mind to make you a present of another humble servant; a fellow that I took up at Lyons, who has served me honestly ever since.

ORIANA

Then why will you part with him?

DUGARD

He has gained so insufferably on my good-humour, that he's grown too familiar; but the fellow's cunning, and may be serviceable to you in your affair with Mirabel. Here he comes.

Enter **PETIT**.

Well, sir, have you been at Rousseau's?

PETIT

Yes, sir, and who should I find there but Mr. Mirabel and the captain, hatching as warmly over a tub of ice, as two hen pheasants over a brood—They would not let me bespeak any thing, for they had dined before I came.

DUGARD

Come, sir, you shall serve my sister, I shall still continue kind to you; and if your lady recommends your diligence, upon trial, I'll use my interest to advance you.—Wait on your lady home, Petit.

[Exit.

PETIT

A chair! a chair! a chair!

ORIANA

No, no, I'll walk home, 'tis but next door.

[Exeunt.

SCENE II.—A Tavern

YOUNG MIRABEL and **DURETETE** discovered, rising from Table.

YOUNG MIRABEL

Welcome to Paris once more, my dear Captain; we have eat heartily, drank roundly, paid plentifully, and let it go for once. I liked every thing but our women; they looked so lean and tawdry, poor creatures! 'Tis a sure sign the army is not paid. Give me the plump Venetian, brisk, and sanguine, that smiles upon me like the glowing sun, and meets my lips like sparkling wine, her person, shining as the glass, and spirit, like the foaming liquor.

DURETTE
Ah, Mirabel, Italy I grant you; but for our women here in France, they are such thin, brawn, fallen jades, a man may as well make a bed-fellow of a cane chair.

YOUNG MIRABEL
France! A light, unseasoned country, nothing but feathers, foppery, and fashions.—There's nothing on this side the Alps worth my humble service t'ye—Ha, Roma la Santa!—Italy for my money!—their customs, gardens, buildings, paintings, music, policies, wine, and women! the paradise of the world!—not pestered with a parcel of precise, old, gouty fellows, that would debar their children every pleasure, that they themselves are past the sense of;—commend me to the Italian familiarity—"Here, son, there's fifty crowns, go, pay your girl her week's allowance."

DURETTE
Ay, these are your fathers, for you, that understand the necessities of young men! not like our musty dads, who, because they cannot fish themselves, would muddy the water, and spoil the sport of them that can. But now you talk of the plump, what d'ye think of a Dutch woman?

YOUNG MIRABEL
A Dutch woman's too compact,—nay, every thing among them is so; a Dutch man is thick, a Dutch woman is squab, a Dutch horse is round, a Dutch dog is short, a Dutch ship is broad bottomed; and, in short, one would swear, that the whole product of the country were cast in the same mould with their cheeses.

DURETTE
Ay, but Mirabel, you have forgot the English ladies.

YOUNG MIRABEL
The women of England were excellent, did they not take such unsufferable pains to ruin, what nature has made so incomparably well; they would be delicate creatures indeed, could they but thoroughly arrive at the French mien, or entirely let it alone; for they only spoil a very good air of their own, by an awkward imitation of ours. But come, Duretete, let us mind the business in hand; Mistresses we must have, and must take up with the manufacture of the place, and upon a competent diligence, we shall find those in Paris shall match the Italians from top to toe.

DURETTE
Ay, Mirabel, you will do well enough, but what will become of your friend? you know, I am so plaguy bashful! so naturally an ass upon these occasions, that—

YOUNG MIRABEL
Pshaw! you must be bolder, man! Travel three years, and bring home such a baby as bashfulness! A great lusty fellow, and a soldier; fie upon it!

DURETTE
Lookye, sir, I can visit, and I can ogle a little,—as thus, or thus now. Then I can kiss abundantly—but if they chance to give me a forbidding look, as some women, you know, have a devilish cast with their

eyes—or if they cry, "What do you mean? what d'ye take me for? Fie, sir, remember who I am, sir—A person of quality to be used at this rate!"—'Egad, I'm struck as flat as a fryingpan.

YOUNG MIRABEL
Words of course! never mind them: Turn you about upon your heel, with a jantée air; hum out the end of an old song; cut a cross caper, and at her again.

DURETTE [Imitates him.]
No, hang it, 'twill never do!—Oons! what did my father mean, by sticking me up in an university, or to think that I should gain any thing by my head, in a nation, whose genius lies all in their heels!—Well, if ever I come to have children of my own, they shall have the education of the country—they shall learn to dance, before they can walk, and be taught to sing, before they can speak.

YOUNG MIRABEL
Come, come, throw off that childish humour—put on assurance, there's no avoiding it; stand all hazards, thou'rt a stout, lusty fellow, and hast a good estate;—look bluff, hector, you have a good side-box face, a pretty impudent face; so, that's pretty well.—This fellow went abroad like an ox, and is returned like an ass. [Aside.

DURETTE
Let me see now, how I look.

[Pulls out a Pocket Glass, and looks on it.]

A side-box face, say you!—'Egad, I don't like it, Mirabel! Fie, sir, don't abuse your friends, I could not wear such a face for the best countess in christendom.

YOUNG MIRABEL
Why can't you, blockhead, as well as I?

DURETTE
Why, thou hast impudence to set a good face upon any thing; I would change half my gold for half thy brass, with all my heart. Who comes here? Odso, Mirabel, your father!

Enter **OLD MIRABEL**.

OLD MIRABEL
Where's Bob?—dear Bob?

YOUNG MIRABEL
Your blessing, sir?

OLD MIRABEL
My blessing! Damn ye, ye young rogue, why did not you come to see your father first, sirrah? My dear boy, I am heartily glad to see thee, my dear child, 'faith!—Captain Duretete, by the blood of the Mirabels, I'm yours! Well, my lads, ye look bravely, 'faith.—Bob, hast got any money left?

YOUNG MIRABEL

Not a farthing, sir.

OLD MIRABEL
Why, then, I won't gi' thee a souse.

YOUNG MIRABEL
I did but jest, here's ten pistoles.

OLD MIRABEL
Why, then, here's ten more: I love to be charitable to those that don't want it.—Well, and how do you like Italy, my boys?

YOUNG MIRABEL
O, the garden of the world, sir! Rome, Naples, Venice, Milan, and a thousand others—all fine.

OLD MIRABEL
Ay! say you so? And they say, that Chiari is very fine too.

DURETTE
Indifferent, sir, very indifferent; a very scurvy air, the most unwholesome to a French constitution in the world.

YOUNG MIRABEL
Pshaw! nothing on't: these rascally gazetteers have misinformed you.

OLD MIRABEL
Misinformed me! Oons, sir, were we not beaten there?

YOUNG MIRABEL
Beaten, sir! we beaten!

OLD MIRABEL
Why, how was it, pray, sweet sir?

YOUNG MIRABEL
Sir, the captain will tell you.

DURETTE
No, sir, your son will tell you.

YOUNG MIRABEL
The captain was in the action, sir.

DURETTE
Your son saw more than I, sir, for he was a looker on.

OLD MIRABEL

Confound you both, for a brace of cowards! here are no Germans to overhear you—why don't ye tell me how it was?

YOUNG MIRABEL

Why, then, you must know, that we marched up a body of the finest, bravest, well dressed fellows in the universe; our commanders at the head of us, all lace and feather, like so many beaux at a ball—I don't believe there was a man of them but could dance a charmer, Morbleau.

OLD MIRABEL

Dance! very well, pretty fellows, 'faith!

YOUNG MIRABEL

We capered up to their very trenches, and there saw, peeping over, a parcel of scare-crow, olive-coloured, gunpowder fellows, as ugly as the devil.

DURETTE

E'gad, I shall never forget the looks of them, while I have breath to fetch.

YOUNG MIRABEL

They were so civil, indeed, as to welcome us with their cannon! but for the rest, we found them such unmannerly, rude, unsociable dogs, that we grew tired of their company, and so we e'en danced back again.

OLD MIRABEL

And did ye all come back?

YOUNG MIRABEL

No, two or three thousand of us staid behind.

OLD MIRABEL

Why, Bob, why?

YOUNG MIRABEL

Pshaw! because they could not come that night.

DURETTE

No, sir, because they could not come that night.

YOUNG MIRABEL

But, come, sir, we were talking of something else; pray, how does your lovely charge, the fair Oriana?

OLD MIRABEL

Ripe, sir, just ripe; you'll find it better engaging with her than with the Germans, let me tell you. And what would you say, my young Mars, if I had a Venus for thee too? Come, Bob, your apartment is ready, and pray let your friend be my guest too; you shall command the house between ye, and I'll be as merry as the best of you.

[Exeunt.

SCENE I.—Old Mirabel's House

ORIANA and **BISARRE**.

BISARRE
And you love this young rake, d'ye?

ORIANA
Yes.

BISARRE
In spite of all his ill usage?

ORIANA
I can't help it.

BISARRE
What's the matter wi' ye?

ORIANA
Pshaw!

BISARRE
Um!—before that any young, lying, swearing, flattering, rakehelly fellow, should play such tricks with me—O, the devil take all your Cassandras and Cleopatras for me.—I warrant now, you'll play the fool when he comes, and say you love him! eh?

ORIANA
Most certainly; I can't dissemble, Bisarre; besides, 'tis past that, we're contracted.

BISARRE
Contracted! alack-a-day, poor thing!—What, you have changed rings, or broken an old broadpiece between you! I would make a fool of any fellow in France. Well, I must confess, I do love a little coquetting, with all my heart! my business should be to break gold with my lover one hour, and crack my promise the next; he should find me one day with a prayer book in my hand, and with a play book another.—He should have my consent to buy the wedding ring, and the next moment would I ask him his name.

ORIANA
O, my dear! were there no greater tie upon my heart, than there is upon my conscience, I would soon throw the contract out of doors; but the mischief on't is, I am so fond of being tied, that I'm forced to be just, and the strength of my passion keeps down the inclination of my sex.

BISARRE
But here's the old gentleman!

Enter **OLD MIRABEL**.

OLD MIRABEL
Where's my wenches?—where's my two little girls? Eh! Have a care,—look to yourselves, 'faith, they're a coming—the travellers are a coming! Well! which of you two will be my daughter-in-law now? Bisarre, Bisarre, what say you, madcap? Mirabel is a pure, wild fellow.

BISARRE
I like him the worse.

OLD MIRABEL
You lie, hussy, you like him the better, indeed you do! What say you, my t'other little filbert, eh?

ORIANA
I suppose the gentleman will chuse for himself, sir.

OLD MIRABEL
Why, that's discreetly said, and so he shall.

Enter **MIRABEL** and **DURETETE**; they salute the **LADIES**.

Bob, harkye, you shall marry one of these girls, sirrah!

YOUNG MIRABEL
Sir, I'll marry them both, if you please.

BISARRE [Aside.]
He'll find that one may serve his turn.

OLD MIRABEL
Both! why, you young dog, d'ye banter me?—Come, sir, take your choice.—Duretete, you shall have your choice too, but Robin shall chuse first.—Come, sir, begin. Well! which d'ye like?

YOUNG MIRABEL
Both.

OLD MIRABEL
But which will you marry?

YOUNG MIRABEL
Neither.

OLD MIRABEL
Neither! Don't make me angry now, Bob—pray, don't make me angry.—Lookye, sirrah, if I don't dance at your wedding to-morrow, I shall be very glad to cry at your grave.

YOUNG MIRABEL

That's a bull, father.

OLD MIRABEL

A bull! Why, how now, ungrateful sir, did I make thee a man, that thou shouldst make me a beast?

YOUNG MIRABEL

Your pardon, sir; I only meant your expression.

OLD MIRABEL

Harkye, Bob, learn better manners to your father before strangers! I won't be angry this time: But oons, if ever you do't again, you rascal!—remember what I say.

[Exit.

YOUNG MIRABEL

Pshaw! what does the old fellow mean by mewing me up here with a couple of green girls?—Come, Duretete, will you go?

ORIANA

I hope, Mr. Mirabel, you han't forgot—

YOUNG MIRABEL

No, no, madam, I han't forgot, I have brought you a thousand little Italian curiosities; I'll assure you, madam, as far as a hundred pistoles would reach, I han't forgot the least circumstance.

ORIANA

Sir, you misunderstand me.

YOUNG MIRABEL

Odso! the relics, madam, from Rome. I do remember, now, you made a vow of chastity before my departure; a vow of chastity, or something like it—was it not, madam?

ORIANA

O sir, I'm answered at present.

[Exit.

YOUNG MIRABEL

She was coming full mouth upon me with her contract—'Would I might despatch t'other!

DURETTE

Mirabel, that lady there, observe her, she's wondrous pretty, 'faith! and seems to have but few words; I like her mainly—speak to her, man, pr'ythee speak to her.

YOUNG MIRABEL

Madam, here's a gentleman, who declares—

DURETTE

Madam, don't believe him, I declare nothing—What, the devil, do you mean, man?

YOUNG MIRABEL

He says, madam, that you are as beautiful as an angel.

DURETTE

He tells a damned lie, madam! I say no such thing—Are you mad, Mirabel? Why, I shall drop down with shame.

YOUNG MIRABEL

And so, madam, not doubting but your ladyship may like him as well as he does you, I think it proper to leave you together.

[Going, **DURETETE** holds him.

DURETTE

Hold, hold—Why, Mirabel, friend, sure you won't be so barbarous as to leave me alone! Pr'ythee, speak to her for yourself, as it were! Lord, Lord, that a Frenchman should want impudence!

YOUNG MIRABEL

You look mighty demure, madam.—She's deaf, Captain.

DURETTE

I had much rather have her dumb.

YOUNG MIRABEL

The gravity of your air, madam, promises some extraordinary fruits from your study, which moves us with curiosity to inquire the subject of your ladyship's contemplation.—Not a word!

DURETTE

I hope in the Lord, she's speechless! if she be, she's mine this moment. Mirabel, d'ye think a woman's silence can be natural?

BISARRE

But the forms which logicians introduce, and which proceed from simple enumeration, are dubitable, and proceed only upon admittance—

YOUNG MIRABEL

Hoyty toyty! what a plague have we here? Plato in petticoats!

DURETTE

Ay, ay, let her go on, man; she talks in my own mother tongue.

BISARRE

'Tis exposed to invalidity, from a contradictory instance; looks only upon common operations, and is infinite in its termination.

YOUNG MIRABEL
Rare pedantry!

DURETTE
Axioms! axioms! self-evident principles!

BISARRE
Then the ideas wherewith the mind is pre-occupate.—O, gentlemen, I hope you'll pardon my cogitation! I was involved in a profound point of philosophy, but I shall discuss it somewhere else, being satisfied, that the subject is not agreeable to your sparks, that profess the vanity of the times.

[Exit.

YOUNG MIRABEL
Go thy way, good wife Bias! Do you hear, Duretete? Dost hear this starched piece of austerity?

DURETTE
She's mine, man, she's mine—My own talent to a T.—I'll match her in dialectics, 'faith! I was seven years at the university, man, nursed up with Barbaro, Celarunt, Darii, Ferio, Baralipton. Did you ever know, man, that 'twas metaphysics made me an ass? It was, 'faith! Had she talked a word of singing, dancing, plays, fashions, or the like, I had foundered at the first step; but as she is—Mirabel, wish me joy!

YOUNG MIRABEL
You don't mean marriage, I hope?

DURETTE
No, no, I am a man of more honour.

YOUNG MIRABEL
Bravely resolved, Captain! now for thy credit—warm me this frozen snowball—'twill be a conquest above the Alps!

DURETTE
But will you promise to be always near me?

YOUNG MIRABEL
Upon all occasions, never fear.

DURETTE
Why, then, you shall see me, in two moments, make an induction from my love to her hand, from her hand to her mouth, from her mouth to her heart, and so conclude in her bed, categorematice.

YOUNG MIRABEL
Now the game begins, and my fool is entered.—But here comes one to spoil my sport; now shall I be teased to death, with this old-fashioned contract! I should love her too, if I might do it my own way, but she'll do nothing without witnesses, forsooth! I wonder women can be so immodest!

Enter **ORIANA**.

Well, madam, why d'ye follow me?

ORIANA
Well, sir, why do you shun me?

YOUNG MIRABEL
'Tis my humour, madam, and I'm naturally swayed by inclination.

ORIANA
Have you forgot our contract, sir?

YOUNG MIRABEL
All I remember of that contract is, that it was made some three years ago, and that's enough, in conscience, to forget the rest on't.

ORIANA
'Tis sufficient, sir, to recollect the passing of it; for, in that circumstance, I presume, lies the force of the obligation.

YOUNG MIRABEL
Obligations, madam, that are forced upon the will, are no tie upon the conscience; I was a slave to my passion, when I passed the instrument, but the recovery of my freedom makes the contract void.

ORIANA
Come, Mr. Mirabel, these expressions I expected from the raillery of your humour, but I hope for very different sentiments from your honour and generosity.

YOUNG MIRABEL
Lookye, madam, as for my generosity, 'tis at your service, with all my heart: I'll keep you a coach and six horses, if you please, only permit me to keep my honour to myself. Consider, madam, you have no such thing among ye, and 'tis a main point of policy to keep no faith with reprobates—thou art a pretty little reprobate, and so get thee about thy business!

ORIANA
Well, sir, even all this I will allow to the gaiety of your temper; your travels have improved your talent of talking, but they are not of force, I hope, to impair your morals.

YOUNG MIRABEL
Morals! why, there 'tis again now!—I tell thee, child, there is not the least occasion for morals, in any business between you and I. Don't you know that, of all commerce in the world, there is no such cozenage and deceit, as in the traffic between man and woman? we study all our lives long, how to put tricks upon one another.—No fowler lays abroad more nets for his game, nor a hunter for his prey, than you do, to catch poor innocent men.—Why do you sit three or four hours at your toilet in a morning? only with a villanous design to make some poor fellow a fool before night. What d'ye sigh for?—What d'ye weep for?—What d'ye pray for? Why, for a husband: That is, you implore Providence to assist you,

in the just, and pious design, of making the wisest of his creatures a fool, and the head of the creation, a slave.

ORIANA
Sir, I am proud of my power, and am resolved to use it.

YOUNG MIRABEL
Hold, hold, madam, not so fast—As you have variety of vanities to make coxcombs of us; so we have vows, oaths, and protestations, of all sorts and sizes, to make fools of you—And this, in short, my dear creature, is our present condition. I have sworn, and lied, briskly, to gain my ends of you; your ladyship has patched and painted violently, to gain your ends of me; but, since we are both disappointed, let us make a drawn battle, and part clear on both sides.

ORIANA
With all my heart, sir! give me up my contract, and I'll never see your face again.

YOUNG MIRABEL
Indeed, I won't, child!

ORIANA
What, sir! neither do one nor t'other?

YOUNG MIRABEL
No, you shall die a maid, unless you please to be otherwise, upon my terms.

ORIANA
What do you intend by this, sir?

YOUNG MIRABEL
Why, to starve you into compliance;—lookye, you shall never marry any man; and you had as good let me do you a kindness as a stranger.

ORIANA
Sir, you're a—

YOUNG MIRABEL
What am I, ma'am?

ORIANA
A villain, sir.

YOUNG MIRABEL
I'm glad on't—I never knew an honest fellow in my life, but was a villain upon these occasions. Han't you drawn yourself, now, into a very pretty dilemma? ha! ha! ha! the poor lady has made a vow of virginity, when she thought of making a vow to the contrary. Was ever poor woman so cheated into chastity?

ORIANA

Sir, my fortune is equal to yours, my friends as powerful, and both shall be put to the test, to do me justice.

YOUNG MIRABEL
What! you'll force me to marry you, will ye?

ORIANA
Sir, the law shall.

YOUNG MIRABEL
But the law can't force me to do any thing else, can it?

ORIANA
Pshaw, I despise thee—Monster!

YOUNG MIRABEL
Kiss and be friends, then—Don't cry, child, and you shall have your sugar plumb—Come, madam, d'ye think I could be so unreasonable as to make you fast all your life long! No, I did but jest, you shall have your liberty—here, take your contract, and give me mine.

ORIANA
No, I won't.

YOUNG MIRABEL
Eh! What, is the girl a fool?

ORIANA
No, sir, you shall find me cunning enough to do myself justice; and since I must not depend upon your love, I'll be revenged, and force you to marry me, out of spite.

YOUNG MIRABEL
Then I'll beat thee out of spite, and make a most confounded husband!

ORIANA
O, sir, I shall match ye! A good husband makes a good wife at any time.

YOUNG MIRABEL
I'll rattle down your china about your ears.

ORIANA
And I'll rattle about the city, to run you in debt for more.

YOUNG MIRABEL
I'll tear the furbelow off your clothes, and when you swoon for vexation, you shan't have a penny, to buy a bottle of hartshorn.

ORIANA
And you, sir, shall have hartshorn in abundance.

YOUNG MIRABEL
I'll keep as many mistresses as I have coach horses.

ORIANA
And I'll keep as many gallants as you have grooms.

YOUNG MIRABEL
But, sweet madam, there is such a thing as a divorce!

ORIANA
But, sweet sir, there is such a thing as alimony! so divorce on, and spare not.

[Exit.

YOUNG MIRABEL
Ay, that separate maintenance is the devil—there's their refuge!—O' my conscience, one would take cuckoldom for a meritorious action, because the women are so handsomely rewarded for it.

[Exit.

Enter **DURETETE** and **PETIT**.

DURETTE
And she's mighty peevish, you say?

PETIT
O sir, she has a tongue as long as my leg, and talks so crabbedly, you would think she always spoke Welsh.

DURETTE
That's an odd language, methinks, for her philosophy.

PETIT
But sometimes she will sit you half a day without speaking a word, and talk oracles all the while by the wrinkles of her forehead, and the motions of her eyebrows.

DURETTE
Nay, I shall match her in philosophical ogles, 'faith!—that's my talent: I can talk best, you must know, when I say nothing.

PETIT
But d'ye ever laugh, sir?

DURETTE
Laugh? Won't she endure laughing?

PETIT

Why, she's a critic, sir, she hates a jest, for fear it should please her; and nothing keeps her in humour, but what gives her the spleen.—And then, for logic, and all that, you know—

DURETTE
Ay, ay, I'm prepared, I have been practising hard words and no sense, this hour, to entertain her.

PETIT
Then place yourself behind this screen, that you may have a view of her behaviour before you begin.

DURETTE
I long to engage her, lest I should forget my lesson.

PETIT
Here she comes, sir—I must fly.

[Exit **PETIT**, and **DURETETE** stands peeping behind the Curtain.

Enter **BISARRE** and **MAID**.

BISARRE [With a Book.]
Pshaw! hang books! they sour our temper, spoil our eyes, and ruin our complexions.

[Throws away the Book.

DURETTE
Eh? the devil such a word there is in all Aristotle!

BISARRE
Come, wench, let's be free—call in the fiddle, there's nobody near us.

DURETTE
'Would to the Lord there was not!

BISARRE
Here, friend, a minuet—[Music.] Quicker time—ha—'would we had a man or two!

DURETTE [Stealing away.]
You shall have the devil sooner, my dear, dancing philosopher!

BISARRE
Uds my life!—Here's one!

[Runs to **DURETETE**, and hales him back.

DURETTE
Is all my learned preparation come to this?

BISARRE

Come, sir, don't be ashamed, that's my good boy—you're very welcome, we wanted such a one—Come, strike up—[Dance.] I know you dance well, sir, you're finely shaped for't—Come, come, sir;—quick, quick! you miss the time else.

DURETTE
But, madam, I come to talk with you.

BISARRE
Ay, ay, talk as you dance, talk as you dance,—come.

DURETTE
But we were talking of dialectics—

BISARRE
Hang dialectics! [Music.] Mind the time—quicker, sirrah!—Come—and how d'ye find yourself now, sir?

DURETTE
In a fine breathing sweat, Doctor.

BISARRE
All the better, patient, all the better;—Come, sir, sing now, sing, I know you sing well: I see you have a singing face—a heavy, dull, sonata face.

DURETTE
Who, I sing?

BISARRE
O you're modest, sir—but come, sit down closer—closer. Here, a bottle of wine!

[Exit **MAID**, and returns with Wine.]

Come, sir—sing, sir.

DURETTE
But, madam, I came to talk with you.

BISARRE
O sir, you shall drink first.—Come, fill me a bumper—here, sir, bless the king!

DURETTE
'Would I were out of his dominions!—By this light, she'll make me drunk too!

BISARRE
O pardon me, sir, you shall do me right—fill it higher.—Now, sir, can you drink a health under your leg?

DURETTE
Rare philosophy that, 'faith!

BISARRE

Come, off with it to the bottom!—Now, how d'ye like me, sir?

DURETTE

O, mighty well, madam!

BISARRE

You see how a woman's fancy varies! sometimes, splenetic and heavy, then, gay and frolicsome.—And how d'ye like the humour?

DURETTE

Good madam, let me sit down to answer you, for I am heartily tired.

BISARRE

Fie upon't! a young man, and tired! up, for shame, and walk about!—Action becomes us—a little faster, sir—What d'ye think now of my Lady La Pale, and Lady Coquet, the duke's fair daughter? Ha! Are they not brisk lasses? Then there is black Mrs. Bellair, and brown Mrs. Bellface!

DURETTE

They are all strangers to me, madam.

BISARRE

But let me tell you, sir, that brown is not always despicable—O Lard, sir, if young Mrs. Bagatell had kept herself single till this time o'day, what a beauty there had been! And then, you know, the charming Mrs. Monkeylove, the fair gem of St. Germain's!

DURETTE

Upon my soul, I don't!

BISARRE

And then, you must have heard of the English beau, Spleenamore, how unlike a gentleman—

DURETTE

Hey!—not a syllable on't, as I hope to be saved, madam!

BISARRE

No! Why, then, play me a jig;—[Music.]—Come, sir.

DURETTE

By this light, I cannot! 'faith, madam, I have sprained my leg!

BISARRE

Then sit you down, sir;—and now tell me what's your business with me? What's your errand? Quick, quick, despatch!—Odso, may be, you are some gentleman's servant, that has brought me a letter, or a haunch of venison?

DURETTE

'Sdeath, madam, do I look like a carrier?

BISARRE

O, cry you mercy, I saw you just now, I mistook you, upon my word! you are one of the travelling gentlemen—and pray, sir, how do all our impudent friends in Italy?

DURETTE

Madam, I came to wait on you with a more serious intention than your entertainment has answered.

BISARRE

Sir, your intention of waiting on me was the greatest affront imaginable, however your expressions may turn it to a compliment: Your visit, sir, was intended as a prologue to a very scurvy play, of which, Mr. Mirabel and you so handsomely laid the plot.—"Marry! No, no, I am a man of more honour."—Where's your honour? Where's your courage now? Ads my life, sir, I have a great mind to kick you!—Go, go to your fellow-rake now, rail at my sex, and get drunk for vexation, and write a lampoon—But I must have you to know, sir, that my reputation is above the scandal of a libel, my virtue is sufficiently approved to those whose opinion is my interest: and, for the rest, let them talk what they will; for, when I please, I'll be what I please, in spite of you and all mankind; and so, my dear man of honour, if you be tired, con over this lesson, and sit there till I come to you.

[Runs off.

DURETTE

Tum ti dum. [Sings.] Ha! ha! ha! "Ad's my life, I have a great mind to kick you!"—Oons and confusion! [Starts up.] Was ever man so abused!—Ay, Mirabel set me on.

Enter **PETIT**.

PETIT

Well, sir, how d'ye find yourself?

DURETTE

You son of a nine-eyed whore, d'ye come to abuse me? I'll kick you with a vengeance, you dog!

[**PETIT** runs off, and **DURETETE** after him.

ACT THE THIRD

SCENE I.—Old Mirabel's House

Enter **OLD MIRABEL** and **YOUNG MIRABEL**, meeting.

OLD MIRABEL

Bob, come hither, Bob.

YOUNG MIRABEL

Your pleasure, sir?

OLD MIRABEL
Are not you a great rogue, sirrah?

YOUNG MIRABEL
That's a little out of my comprehension, sir; for I've heard say, that I resemble my father.

OLD MIRABEL
Your father is your very humble slave—I tell thee what, child, thou art a very pretty fellow, and I love thee heartily; and a very great villain, and I hate thee mortally.

YOUNG MIRABEL
Villain, sir! Then I must be a very impudent one; for I can't recollect any passage of my life that I'm ashamed of.

OLD MIRABEL
Come hither, my dear friend; dost see this picture?

[Shows him a little Picture.

YOUNG MIRABEL
Oriana's? Pshaw!

OLD MIRABEL
What, sir, won't you look upon't?—Bob, dear Bob, pr'ythee come hither now—Dost want any money, child?

YOUNG MIRABEL
No, sir.

OLD MIRABEL
Why, then, here's some for thee: come here now—How canst thou be so hard-hearted, an unnatural, unmannerly rascal, don't mistake me, child, I a'n't angry, as to abuse this tender, lovely, good-natured, dear rogue?—Why, she sighs for thee, and cries for thee, pouts for thee, and snubs for thee; the poor little heart of it is like to burst—Come, my dear boy, be good-natured, like your own father; be now—and then, see here, read this—the effigies of the lovely Oriana, with thirty thousand pound to her portion—thirty thousand pound, you dog! thirty thousand pound, you rogue! how dare you refuse a lady with thirty thousand pound, you impudent rascal?

YOUNG MIRABEL
Will you hear me speak, sir?

OLD MIRABEL
Hear you speak, sir! If you had thirty thousand tongues, you could not out-talk thirty thousand pound, sir.

YOUNG MIRABEL

Nay, sir, if you won't hear me, I'll begone, sir! I'll take post for Italy this moment.

OLD MIRABEL
Ah, the fellow knows I won't part with him! Well, sir, what have you to say?

YOUNG MIRABEL
The universal reception, sir, that marriage has had in the world, is enough to fix it for a public good, and to draw every body into the common cause; but there are some constitutions, like some instruments, so peculiarly singular, that they make tolerable music by themselves, but never do well in a concert.

OLD MIRABEL
Why, this is reason, I must confess, but yet it is nonsense too; for, though you should reason like an angel, if you argue yourself out of a good estate, you talk like a fool.

YOUNG MIRABEL
But, sir, if you bribe me into bondage with the riches of Croesus, you leave me but a beggar, for want of my liberty.

OLD MIRABEL
Was ever such a perverse fool heard? 'Sdeath, sir! why did I give you education? was it to dispute me out of my senses? Of what colour, now, is the head of this cane? You'll say, 'tis white, and, ten to one, make me believe it too—I thought that young fellows studied to get money.

YOUNG MIRABEL
No, sir, I have studied to despise it; my reading was not to make me rich, but happy, sir.

OLD MIRABEL
There he has me again, now! But, sir, did not I marry to oblige you?

YOUNG MIRABEL
To oblige me, sir! in what respect, pray?

OLD MIRABEL
Why, to bring you into the world, sir; wa'n't that an obligation?

YOUNG MIRABEL
And, because I would have it still an obligation, I avoid marriage.

OLD MIRABEL
How is that, sir?

YOUNG MIRABEL
Because I would not curse the hour I was born.

OLD MIRABEL
Lookye, friend, you may persuade me out of my designs, but I'll command you out of yours; and, though you may convince my reason that you are in the right, yet there is an old attendant of sixty-three, called

positiveness, which you, nor all the wits in Italy, shall ever be able to shake: so, sir, you're a wit, and I'm a father: you may talk, but I'll be obeyed.

YOUNG MIRABEL
This it is to have the son a finer gentleman than the father; they first give us breeding, that they don't understand; then they turn us out of doors, because we are wiser than themselves. But I'm a little aforehand with the old gentleman. [Aside.] Sir, you have been pleased to settle a thousand pound sterling a year upon me; in return of which, I have a very great honour for you and your family, and shall take care that your only and beloved son shall do nothing to make him hate his father, or to hang himself. So, dear sir, I'm your very humble servant.

[Runs off.

OLD MIRABEL
Here, sirrah! rogue! Bob! villain!

Enter **DUGARD**.

DUGARD
Ah, sir! 'tis but what he deserves.

OLD MIRABEL
'Tis false, sir! he don't deserve it: what have you to say against my boy, sir?

DUGARD
I shall only repeat your own words.

OLD MIRABEL
What have you to do with my words? I have swallowed my words already; I have eaten them up.—I say, that Bob's an honest fellow, and who dares deny it?

Enter **BISARRE**.

BISARRE
That dare I, sir:—I say, that your son is a wild, foppish, whimsical, impertinent coxcomb; and, were I abused, as this gentleman's sister is, I would make it an Italian quarrel, and poison the whole family.

DUGARD
Come, sir, 'tis no time for trifling: my sister is abused; you are made sensible of the affront, and your honour is concerned to see her redressed.

OLD MIRABEL
Lookye, Mr. Dugard, good words go farthest. I will do your sister justice, but it must be after my own rate; nobody must abuse my son but myself; for, although Robin be a sad dog, yet he's nobody's puppy but my own.

BISARRE

Ay, that's my sweet-natured, kind, old gentleman—[Wheedling him.] We will be good, then, if you'll join with us in the plot.

OLD MIRABEL
Ah, you coaxing young baggage! what plot can you have to wheedle a fellow of sixty-three?

BISARRE
A plot that sixty-three is only good for; to bring other people together, sir. You must act the Spaniard, because your son will least suspect you; and, if he should, your authority protects you from a quarrel, to which Oriana is unwilling to expose her brother.

OLD MIRABEL
And what part will you act in the business, madam?

BISARRE
Myself, sir; my friend is grown a perfect changeling: these foolish hearts of ours spoil our heads presently; the fellows no sooner turn knaves, but we turn fools: but I am still myself, and he may expect the most severe usage from me, because I neither love him, nor hate him.

[Exit.

OLD MIRABEL
Well said, Mrs. Paradox! but, sir, who must open the matter to him?

DUGARD
Petit, sir; who is our engineer general; and here he comes.

Enter **PETIT**.

PETIT
O, sir, more discoveries! are all friends about us?

DUGARD
Ay, ay, speak freely.

PETIT
You must know, sir,—od's my life, I'm out of breath! You must know, sir,—you must know—

OLD MIRABEL
What the devil must we know, sir?

PETIT
That I have [Pants and blows.] bribed, sir, bribed—your son's secretary of state.

OLD MIRABEL
Secretary of state!—who's that, for Heaven's sake?

PETIT

His valet de chambre, sir? You must know, sir, that the intrigue lay folded up in his master's clothes; and, when he went to dust the embroidered suit, the secret flew out of the right pocket of his coat, in a whole swarm of your crambo songs, short-footed odes, and long-legged pindarics.

OLD MIRABEL
Impossible!

PETIT
Ah, sir, he has loved her all along; there was Oriana in every line, but he hates marriage. Now, sir, this plot will stir up his jealousy, and we shall know, by the strength of that, how to proceed farther.

Come, sir, let's about it with speed:
'Tis expedition gives our king the sway;
For expedition to the French give way;
Swift to attack, or swift—to run away.

[Exeunt.

Enter **YOUNG MIRABEL** and **BISARRE**, passing carelessly by one another.

BISARRE [Aside.]
I wonder what she can see in this fellow, to like him?

YOUNG MIRABEL [Aside.]
I wonder what my friend can see in this girl, to admire her?

BISARRE [Aside.]
A wild, foppish, extravagant, rake-hell!

YOUNG MIRABEL [Aside.]
A light, whimsical, impertinent, madcap!

BISARRE
Whom do you mean, sir?

YOUNG MIRABEL
Whom do you mean, madam?

BISARRE
A fellow, that has nothing left to re-establish him for a human creature, but a prudent resolution to hang himself!

YOUNG MIRABEL
There is a way, madam, to force me to that resolution.

BISARRE
I'll do it, with all my heart.

YOUNG MIRABEL

Then you must marry me.

BISARRE

Lookye, sir, don't think your ill manners to me, shall excuse your ill usage of my friend; nor, by fixing a quarrel here, to divert my zeal for the absent; for I'm resolved, nay, I come prepared, to make you a panegyric, that shall mortify your pride, like any modern dedication.

YOUNG MIRABEL

And I, madam, like a true modern patron, shall hardly give you thanks for your trouble.

BISARRE

Come, sir, to let you see what little foundation you have for your dear sufficiency, I'll take you to pieces.

YOUNG MIRABEL

And what piece will you chuse?

BISARRE

Your heart, to be sure; because I should get presently rid on't: your courage I would give to a Hector, your wit to a lewd playmaker, your honour to an attorney, your body to the physicians, and your soul to its master.

YOUNG MIRABEL

I had the oddest dream last night of the Duchess of Burgundy; methought the furbelows of her gown were pinned up so high behind, that I could not see her head for her tail.

BISARRE

The creature don't mind me! do you think, sir, that your humorous impertinence can divert me? No, sir, I'm above any pleasure that you can give, but that of seeing you miserable. And mark me, sir, my friend, my injured friend, shall yet be doubly happy, and you shall be a husband, as much as the rites of marriage, and the breach of them, can make you.

[Here **YOUNG MIRABEL** pulls out a Virgil, and reads to himself, while she speaks.

YOUNG MIRABEL [Reading.]
At Regina dolos, (quis fallere possit amantem?)
Dissimulare etiam sperásti, perfide tantum—
Very true.
Posse nefas.
By your favour, friend Virgil, 'twas but a rascally trick of your hero, to forsake poor pug so inhumanly.

BISARRE

I don't know what to say to him. The devil—what's Virgil to us, sir?

YOUNG MIRABEL

Very much, madam; the most apropos in the world—for, what should I chop upon, but the very place where the perjured rogue of a lover, and the forsaken lady, are battling it tooth and nail! Come, madam,

spend your spirits no longer; we'll take an easier method: I'll be Æneas now, and you shall be Dido, and we'll rail by book. Now for you, Madam Dido: Nec te noster amor, nec te data dextera quondam, Nec Meritura tenet crudeli funere Dido—
Ah, poor Dido!

[Looking at her.

BISARRE
Rudeness! affronts! impatience! I could almost start out, even to manhood, and want but a weapon, as long as his, to fight him upon the spot. What shall I say?

YOUNG MIRABEL
Now she rants.
Quæ quibus anteferam? jam jam nec Maxima Juno.

BISARRE
A man! No, the woman's birth was spirited away.

YOUNG MIRABEL
Right, right, madam, the very words.

BISARRE
And some pernicious elf left in the cradle, with human shape, to palliate growing mischief.

[Both speak together, and raise their Voices by Degrees.

YOUNG MIRABEL
Perfide, sed duris genuit te Cautibus horrens
Caucasus, Hyrcanæque admorunt Ubera Tigres.

BISARRE
Go, sir, fly to your midnight revels—

YOUNG MIRABEL
Excellent!
I sequere Italiam ventis, pete regna per undas,
Spero equidem mediis, si quid pia Numina possunt.

[Together again.

BISARRE
Converse with imps of darkness of your make; your nature starts at justice, and shivers at the touch of virtue.—Now, the devil take his impudence! He vexes me so, I don't know whether to cry or laugh at him.

YOUNG MIRABEL
Bravely performed, my dear Libyan! I'll write the tragedy of Dido, and you shall act the part; but you do nothing at all, unless you fret yourself into a fit; for here the poor lady is stifled with vapours, drops into

the arms of her maids, and the cruel, barbarous, deceitful, wanderer, is, in the very next line, called pious Æneas.—There's authority for ye.

Sorry indeed Æneas stood,
To see her in a pout;
But Jove himself, who ne'er thought good
To stay a second bout,
Commands him off, with all his crew,
And leaves poor Dy, as I leave you.

[Runs off.

BISARRE
Go thy ways, for a dear, mad, deceitful, agreeable fellow! O' my conscience, I must excuse Oriana.

That lover soon his angry fair disarms,
Whose slighting pleases, and whose faults are charms.

[Exit.

Enter **PETIT**; runs about to every Door, and knocks.

PETIT
Mr. Mirabel! Sir, where are you? no where to be found?

Enter **YOUNG MIRABEL**.

YOUNG MIRABEL
What's the matter, Petit?

PETIT
Most critically met!—Ah, sir, that one who has followed the game so long, and brought the poor hare just under his paws, should let a mungrel cur chop in, and run away with the puss!

YOUNG MIRABEL
If your worship can get out of your allegories, be pleased to tell me, in three words, what you mean.

PETIT
Plain, plain, sir! Your mistress and mine is going to be married!

YOUNG MIRABEL
I believe you lie, sir.

PETIT
Your humble servant, sir.

[Going.

YOUNG MIRABEL
Come hither, Petit. Married, say you?

PETIT
No, sir, 'tis no matter: I only thought to do you a service; but I shall take care how I confer my favours for the future.

YOUNG MIRABEL
Sir, I beg ten thousand pardons.

[Bowing low.

PETIT
'Tis enough, sir.—I come to tell you, sir, that Oriana is this moment to be sacrificed; married past redemption!

YOUNG MIRABEL
I understand her; she'll take a husband, out of spite to me, and then, out of love to me, she will make him a cuckold! But who is the happy man?

PETIT
A lord, sir.

YOUNG MIRABEL
I'm her ladyship's most humble servant. Now must I be a constant attender at my lord's levee, to work my way to my lady's couchee—A countess, I presume, sir—

PETIT
A Spanish count, sir, that Mr. Dugard knew abroad, is come to Paris, saw your mistress yesterday, marries her to-day, and whips her into Spain to-morrow.

YOUNG MIRABEL
Ay, is it so? and must I follow my cuckold over the Pyrenees? Had she married within the precincts of a billet-doux, I would be the man to lead her to church; but, as it happens, I'll forbid the banns! Where is this mighty don?

PETIT
Have a care, sir; he's a rough cross-grained piece, and there's no tampering with him. Would you apply to Mr. Dugard, or the lady herself, something might be done, for it is in despite to you, that the business is carried so hastily. Odso, sir, here he comes! I must be gone.

[Exit.

Enter **OLD MIRABEL**, dressed in a Spanish Habit, leading **ORIANA**.

ORIANA

Good my lord, a nobler choice had better suited your lordship's merit. My person, rank, and circumstance, expose me as the public theme of raillery, and subject me so to injurious usage, my lord, that I can lay no claim to any part of your regard, except your pity.

OLD MIRABEL
Breathes he vital air, that dares presume,
With rude behaviour, to profane such excellence?
Show me the man—
And you shall see how my sudden revenge
Shall fall upon the head of such presumption.
Is this thing one?

[Strutting up to **YOUNG MIRABEL**.

YOUNG MIRABEL
Sir!

ORIANA
Good my lord.

OLD MIRABEL
If he, or any he!

ORIANA
Pray, my lord, the gentleman's a stranger.

OLD MIRABEL
O, your pardon, sir,—but if you had—remember, sir,—the lady now is mine, her injuries are mine; therefore, sir, you understand me—Come, madam.

[Leads **ORIANA** to the Door; she goes off; **YOUNG MIRABEL** runs to his **FATHER**, and pulls him by the Sleeve.

YOUNG MIRABEL
Ecoute, Monsieur le Count.

OLD MIRABEL
Your business, sir?

YOUNG MIRABEL
Boh!

OLD MIRABEL
Boh! what language is that, sir?

YOUNG MIRABEL
Spanish, my lord.

OLD MIRABEL
What d'ye mean?

YOUNG MIRABEL
This, sir.

[Trips up his Heels.

OLD MIRABEL
A very concise quarrel, truly—I'll bully him.—Trinidade Seigneur, give me fair play.

[Offering to rise.

YOUNG MIRABEL
By all means, sir.

[Takes away his Sword.]

Now, seigneur, where's that bombast look, and fustian face, your countship wore just now?

[Strikes him.

OLD MIRABEL
The rogue quarrels well, very well; my own son right!—But hold, sirrah, no more jesting; I'm your father, sir! your father!

YOUNG MIRABEL
My father! Then, by this light, I could find in my heart to pay thee. [Aside.] Is the fellow mad? Why, sure, sir, I han't frighted you out of your senses?

OLD MIRABEL
But you have, sir!

YOUNG MIRABEL
Then I'll beat them into you again.

[Offers to strike him.

OLD MIRABEL
Why, rogue!—Bob! dear Bob! don't you know me, child?

YOUNG MIRABEL
Ha! ha! ha! the fellow's downright distracted! Thou miracle of impudence! wouldst thou make me believe, that such a grave gentleman as my father would go a masquerading thus? That a person of threescore and three would run about, in a fool's coat, to disgrace himself and family? why, you impudent villain, do you think I will suffer such an affront to pass upon my honoured father, my worthy father, my dear father? 'Sdeath, sir! mention my father but once again, and I'll send your soul to thy grandfather this minute!

[Offering to stab him.

OLD MIRABEL
Well, well, I am not your father.

YOUNG MIRABEL
Why, then, sir, you are the saucy, hectoring Spaniard, and I'll use you accordingly.

Enter **DUGARD, ORIANA, MAID**, and **PETIT. DUGARD** runs to **YOUNG MIRABEL**, the rest to the Old Gentleman.

DUGARD
Fie, fie, Mirabel! murder your father!

YOUNG MIRABEL
My father? What, is the whole family mad? Give me way, sir, I won't be held.

OLD MIRABEL
No? nor I neither; let me begone, pray.

[Offering to go.

YOUNG MIRABEL
My father!

OLD MIRABEL
Ay, you dog's face! I am your father, for I have borne as much for thee, as your mother ever did.

YOUNG MIRABEL
O ho! then this was a trick, it seems, a design, a contrivance, a stratagem!—Oh, how my bones ache!

OLD MIRABEL
Your bones, sirrah! why yours?

YOUNG MIRABEL
Why sir, han't I been beating my own flesh and blood all this while? O, madam, [To **ORIANA**.] I wish your ladyship joy of your new dignity. Here was a contrivance indeed!

ORIANA
Pray, sir, don't insult the misfortunes of your own creating.

DUGARD
My prudence will be counted cowardice, if I stand tamely now.—

[Comes up between **YOUNG MIRABEL** and his **SISTER**.]

Well, sir!

YOUNG MIRABEL
Well, sir! Do you take me for one of your tenants, sir, that you put on your landlord's face at me?

DUGARD
On what presumption, sir, dare you assume thus?

[Draws.

OLD MIRABEL
What's that to you, sir?

[Draws.

PETIT
Help! help! the lady faints!

[**ORIANA** falls into her **MAID'S** Arms.

YOUNG MIRABEL
Vapours! vapours! she'll come to herself: If it be an angry fit, a dram of assa foetida—If jealousy, hartshorn in water—if the mother, burnt feathers—If grief, ratafia—If it be straight stays, or corns, there's nothing like a dram of plain brandy.

[Exit.

ORIANA
Hold off, give me air—O, my brother! would you preserve my life, endanger not your own; would you defend my reputation, leave it to itself; 'tis a dear vindication that's purchased by the sword; for, though our champion proves victorious, yet our honour is wounded.

OLD MIRABEL
Ay, and your lover may be wounded, that's another thing. But I think you are pretty brisk again, my child.

ORIANA
Ay, sir, my indisposition was only a pretence to divert the quarrel; the capricious taste of your sex, excuses this artifice in ours.

[Exit.

PETIT
Come, Mr. Dugard, take courage; there is a way still left to fetch him again.

OLD MIRABEL
Sir, I'll have no plot that has any relation to Spain.

DUGARD

I scorn all artifice whatsoever; my sword shall do her justice.

PETIT
Pretty justice, truly! Suppose you run him through the body, you run her through the heart at the same time.

OLD MIRABEL
And me through the head—rot your sword, sir, we'll have plots! Come, Petit, let's hear.

PETIT
What if she pretended to go into a nunnery, and so bring him about to declare himself?

DUGARD
That, I must confess, has a face.

OLD MIRABEL
A face! a face like an angel, sir! Ad's my life, sir, 'tis the most beautiful plot in Christendom! We'll about it immediately.

[Exeunt.

ACT THE FOURTH

SCENE I.—Old Mirabel's House

Enter **OLD MIRABEL** and **DUGARD**.

DUGARD
The Lady Abbess is my relation, and privy to the plot.

OLD MIRABEL
Ay, ay, this nunnery will bring him about, I warrant ye.

Enter **DURETETE**.

DURETTE
Here, where are ye all?—O, Mr. Mirabel! you have done fine things for your posterity—And you, Mr. Dugard, may come to answer this—I come to demand my friend at your hands; restore him, sir, or—[To **OLD MIRABEL**.

OLD MIRABEL
Restore him! What, d'ye think I have got him in my trunk, or my pocket?

DURETTE
Sir, he's mad, and you are the cause on't.

OLD MIRABEL

That may be; for I was as mad as he when I begot him.

DUGARD

Mad, sir! What d'ye mean?

DURETTE

What do you mean, sir, by shutting up your sister, yonder, to talk like a parrot through a cage? or a decoy-duck, to draw others into the snare? Your son, sir, because she has deserted him, he has forsaken the world; and, in three words, has—

OLD MIRABEL

Hanged himself!

DURETTE

The very same—turned friar!

OLD MIRABEL

You lie, sir! 'tis ten times worse. Bob turned friar!—Why should the fellow shave his foolish crown, when the same razor may cut his throat?

DURETTE

If you have any command, or you any interest over him, lose not a minute: He has thrown himself into the next monastery, and has ordered me to pay off his servants, and discharge his equipage.

OLD MIRABEL

Let me alone to ferret him out: I'll sacrifice the Abbot, if he receives him; I'll try whether the spiritual or the natural father has the most right to the child.—But, dear Captain, what has he done with his estate?

DURETTE

Settled it upon the church, sir.

OLD MIRABEL

The church! Nay, then the devil won't get him out of their clutches—Ten thousand livres a year upon the church!—'Tis downright sacrilege—Come, gentlemen, all hands to work: for half that sum, one of these monasteries shall protect you a traitor from the law, a rebellious wife from her husband, and a disobedient son from his own father.

[Exit.

DUGARD

But will ye persuade me that he's gone to a monastery?

DURETTE

Is your sister gone to the Filles Repenties? I tell you, sir, she's not fit for the society of repenting maids.

DUGARD

Why so, sir?

DURETTE
Because she's neither one nor t'other; she's too old to be a maid, and too young to repent.

[Exit—DUGARD after him.

SCENE II.—The Inside of a Monastery

Enter **ORIANA**, in a Nun's Habit, and **BISARRE**.

ORIANA
I hope, Bisarre, there is no harm in jesting with this religious habit.

BISARRE
To me, the greatest jest in the habit, is taking it in earnest.

ORIANA
But I'm reconciled, methinks, to the mortification of a nunnery; because I fancy the habit becomes me.

BISARRE
A well-contrived mortification, truly, that makes a woman look ten times handsomer than she did before!—Ay, my dear, were there any religion in becoming dress, our sex's devotion were rightly placed; for our toilets would do the work of the altar; we should all be canonized.

ORIANA
But don't you think there is a great deal of merit in dedicating a beautiful face and person to the service of religion?

BISARRE
Not half so much as devoting them to a pretty fellow. Come, come, mind your business. Mirabel loves you, 'tis now plain, and hold him to't; give fresh orders that he shan't see you: we get more by hiding our faces, sometimes, than by exposing them; a very mask, you see, whets desire; but a pair of keen eyes, through an iron grate, fire double upon them, with view and disguise. But I must begone upon my affairs; I have brought my captain about again.

ORIANA
But why will you trouble yourself with that coxcomb?

BISARRE
Because he is a coxcomb: had I not better have a lover like him, that I can make an ass of, than a lover like yours, to make a fool of me.

[Knocking below.]

A message from Mirabel, I'll lay my life!

[She runs to the Door.]

Come hither! run, thou charming nun, come hither!

ORIANA
What's the news?

[Runs to her.

BISARRE
Don't you see who's below?

ORIANA
I see nobody but a friar.

BISARRE
Ah, thou poor blind Cupid! A friar! Don't you see a villanous genteel mien, under that cloak of hypocrisy?

ORIANA
As I live, Mirabel turned friar! I hope, in Heaven, he's not in earnest.

BISARRE
In earnest! Ha! ha! ha! are you in earnest? Remember what I say, if you would yield to advantage, and hold out the attack; to draw him on, keep him off, to be sure.

The cunning gamesters never gain too fast,
But lose at first, to win the more at last.

[Exit.

Enter **YOUNG MIRABEL**, in a Friar's Habit.

YOUNG MIRABEL
'Save you, sister—Your brother, young lady, having a regard for your soul's health, has sent me to prepare you for the sacred habit, by confession.

ORIANA
My brother's care I own; and to you, sacred sir, I confess, that the great crying sin, which I have long indulged, and now prepare to expiate, was love. My morning thoughts, my evening prayers, my daily musings, nightly cares, was love!

YOUNG MIRABEL
She's downright stark mad in earnest! Death and confusion, I have lost her! [Aside.]—You confess your fault, madam, in such moving terms, that I could almost be in love with the sin.

ORIANA
Take care, sir; crimes, like virtues, are their own rewards; my chief delight became my only grief; he, in whose breast I thought my heart secure, turned robber, and despoiled the treasure that he kept.

YOUNG MIRABEL
Perhaps that treasure he esteemed so much, that, like the miser, though afraid to use it, he reserves it safe.

ORIANA
No, holy father: who can be miser in another's wealth, that's prodigal of his own? His heart was open, shared to all he knew, and what, alas! must then become of mine! But the same eyes, that drew this passion in, shall send it out in tears, to which now hear my vow—

YOUNG MIRABEL [Discovering himself.]
No, my fair angel! Here, on my knees, behold the criminal, that vows repentance his.

[Kneels.]

Ha! No concern upon her!

Enter **OLD MIRABEL**.

OLD MIRABEL
Where, where's this counterfeit nun?

ORIANA
Madness! confusion! I'm ruined!

YOUNG MIRABEL
What do I hear?

[Puts on his Hood.]

What did you say, sir?

OLD MIRABEL
I say she's a counterfeit, and you may be another, for aught I know, sir: I have lost my child by these tricks, sir.

YOUNG MIRABEL
What tricks, sir?

OLD MIRABEL
By a pretended trick, sir. A contrivance to bring my son to reason, and it has made him stark mad; I have lost him, and a thousand pound a year.

YOUNG MIRABEL [Discovering himself.]
My dear father, I'm your most humble servant.

OLD MIRABEL
My dear boy!

[Runs and kisses him.]

—Welcome, ex inferis, my dear boy! 'tis all a trick, she's no more a nun than I am.

YOUNG MIRABEL
No!

OLD MIRABEL
The devil a bit.

YOUNG MIRABEL
Then kiss me again, my dear dad, for the most happy news—And now, most venerable holy sister,

[Kneels.

Your mercy and your pardon I implore,
For the offence of asking it before.

Lookye, my dear counterfeiting nun, take my advice, be a nun in good earnest; women make the best nuns always, when they can't do otherwise.

ORIANA
O, sir! how unhappily have you destroyed what was so near perfection! He is the counterfeit, that has deceived you.

OLD MIRABEL
Ha! Lookye, sir, I recant; she is a nun.

YOUNG MIRABEL
Sir, your humble servant; then I'm a friar this moment.

OLD MIRABEL
Was ever an old fool so bantered by a brace o' young ones! Hang you both! you're both counterfeits, and my plot's spoiled, that's all.

ORIANA
Shame and confusion, love, anger, and disappointment, will work my brain to madness!

[Takes off her Habit—Exit.

YOUNG MIRABEL
Ay, ay, throw by the rags; they have served a turn for us both, and they shall e'en go off together.

[Takes off his Habit.

[Exit, throwing away the Habit.

Enter **DURETETE**, with a Letter.

DURETTE [Reads.]
My rudeness was only a proof of your humour, which I have found so agreeable, that I own myself penitent, and willing to make any reparation upon your first appearance to Bisarre.

Mirabel swears she loves me, and this confirms it; then farewell gallantry, and welcome revenge! 'Tis my turn now to be upon the sublime; I'll take her off; I warrant her!

Enter **BISARRE.**

Well, mistress, do you love me?

BISARRE
I hope, sir, you will pardon the modesty of—

DURETTE
Of what? of a dancing devil!—Do you love me, I say?

BISARRE
Perhaps I—

DURETTE
What?

BISARRE
Perhaps I do not.

DURETTE
Ha! abused again! Death, woman, I'll—

BISARRE
Hold, hold, sir! I do, do!

DURETTE
Confirm it, then, by your obedience; stand there, and ogle me now, as if your heart, blood, and soul, were like to fly out at your eyes—First, the direct surprise. [She looks full upon him.] Right; next, the deux yeux par oblique. [She gives him the side Glance.] Right; now depart, and languish. [She turns from him, and looks over her Shoulder.] Very well; now sigh. [She sighs.] Now drop your fan on purpose. [She drops her Fan.] Now take it up again. Come now, confess your faults; are not you a proud—say after me.

BISARRE
Proud.

DURETTE
Impertinent.

BISARRE
Impertinent.

DURETTE
Ridiculous.

BISARRE
Ridiculous.

DURETTE
Flirt.

BISARRE
Puppy.

DURETTE
Zoons! Woman, don't provoke me; we are alone, and you don't know but the devil may tempt me to do you a mischief; ask my pardon immediately.

BISARRE
I do, sir; I only mistook the word.

DURETTE
Cry, then. Have you got e'er a handkerchief?

BISARRE
Yes, sir.

DURETTE
Cry, then, handsomely; cry like a queen in a tragedy.

[She pretending to cry, bursts out a laughing.

Enter Two **LADIES**, laughing.

BISARRE
Ha! ha! ha!

Both **LADIES**
Ha! ha! ha!

DURETTE
Hell broke loose upon me, and all the furies fluttered about my ears! Betrayed again?

BISARRE

That you are, upon my word, my dear Captain; ha! ha! ha!

DURETTE
The Lord deliver me!

1ST LADY
What! is this the mighty man, with the bull-face, that comes to frighten ladies?

DURETTE
Ah, madam, I'm the best natured fellow in the world.

BISARRE
A man! we're mistaken; a man has manners: the awkward creature is some tinker's trull, in a periwig. Come, ladies, let us examine him.

[They lay hold on him.

DURETTE
Examine! the devil you will!

BISARRE
I'll lay my life, some great dairy maid in man's clothes!

DURETTE
They will do't;—lookye, dear christian women! pray hear me.

BISARRE
Will you ever attempt a lady's honour again?

DURETTE
If you please to let me get away with my honour, I'll do any thing in the world.

BISARRE
Will you persuade your friend to marry mine?

DURETTE
O yes, to be sure.

BISARRE
And will you do the same by me?

DURETTE
Burn me if I do, if the coast be clear.

[Runs out.

BISARRE
Ha! ha! ha! The visit, ladies, was critical for our diversions: we'll go make an end of our tea.

[Exeunt.

Enter **YOUNG MIRABEL** and **OLD MIRABEL**.

YOUNG MIRABEL
Your patience, sir. I tell you, I won't marry; and, though you send all the bishops in France to persuade me, I shall never believe their doctrine against their practice. You would compel me to that state, which I have heard you curse yourself, when my mother and you have battled it for a whole week together.

OLD MIRABEL
Never but once, you rogue, and that was when she longed for six Flanders mares: ay, sir, then she was breeding of you, which showed what an expensive dog I should have of you.

Enter **PETIT**.

Well, Petit, how does she now?

PETIT
Mad, sir, con pompos—Ay, Mr. Mirabel, you'll believe that I speak truth, now, when I confess that I have told you hitherto nothing but lies: our jesting is come to a sad earnest; she's downright distracted!

Enter **BISARRE**.

BISARRE
Where is this mighty victor!—The great exploit is done. O, sir, [To the old Gentleman.] your wretched ward has found a tender guardian of you, where her young innocence expected protection, here has she found her ruin.

OLD MIRABEL
Ay, the fault is mine; for I believe that rogue won't marry, for fear of begetting such another disobedient son as his father did. I have done all I can, madam, and now can do no more than run mad for company.

[Cries.

Enter **DUGARD**, with his Sword drawn.

DUGARD
Away! Revenge! Revenge!

OLD MIRABEL
Patience! Patience, sir! [**OLD MIRABEL** holds him.] Bob, draw. [Aside.

DUGARD
Patience! the coward's virtue, and the brave man's failing, when thus provoked—Villain!

YOUNG MIRABEL

Your sister's phrensy shall excuse your madness; and, to show my concern for what she suffers, I'll bear the villain from her brother.—Put up your anger with your sword; I have a heart like yours, that swells at an affront received, but melts at an injury given; and, if the lovely Oriana's grief be such a moving scene, 'twill find a part within this breast, perhaps as tender as a brother's.

DUGARD
To prove that soft compassion for her grief, endeavour to remove it.—There, there, behold an object that's infective; I cannot view her, but I am as mad as she!

Enter **ORIANA**, held by Two **MAIDS**, who put her in a Chair.

A sister, that my dying parents left, with their last words and blessing, to my care. Sister, dearest sister!

[Goes to her.

OLD MIRABEL
Ay, poor child, poor child, d'ye know me?

ORIANA
You! you are Amadis de Gaul, sir.—Oh! oh, my heart! Were you never in love, fair lady? And do you never dream of flowers and gardens?—I dream of walking fires, and tall gigantic sights. Take heed, it comes now—What's that? Pray stand away: I have seen that face, sure.—How light my head is!

YOUNG MIRABEL
What piercing charms has beauty, even in madness!

ORIANA
I cannot; for I must be up to go to church, and I must dress me, put on my new gown, and be so fine, to meet my love. Heigho!—Will not you tell me where my heart lies buried?

YOUNG MIRABEL
My very soul is touch'd—Your hand, my fair!

ORIANA
How soft and gentle you feel! I'll tell you your fortune,
friend.

YOUNG MIRABEL
How she stares upon me!

ORIANA
You have a flattering face; but 'tis a fine one—I warrant you have five hundred mistresses—Ay, to be sure, a mistress for every guinea in his pocket—Will you pray for me? I shall die to-morrow—And will you ring my passing bell?

YOUNG MIRABEL
Do you know me, injured creature?

ORIANA
No,—but you shall be my intimate acquaintance—in the grave.

[Weeps.

YOUNG MIRABEL
Oh, tears! I must believe you; sure there's a kind of sympathy in madness; for even I, obdurate as I am, do feel my soul so tossed with storms of passion, that I could cry for help as well as she.

[Wipes his Eyes.

ORIANA
What, have you lost your lover? No, you mock me; I'll go home and pray.

YOUNG MIRABEL
Stay, my fair innocence, and hear me own my love so loud, that I may call your senses to their place, restore them to their charming happy functions, and reinstate myself into your favour.

BISARRE
Let her alone, sir; 'tis all too late: she trembles; hold her, her fits grow stronger by her talking; don't trouble her, she don't know you, sir.

OLD MIRABEL
Not know him! what then? she loves to see him for all that.

Enter **DURETETE**.

DURETTE
Where are you all? What the devil! melancholy, and I here! Are ye sad, and such a ridiculous subject, such a very good jest among you as I am?

YOUNG MIRABEL
Away with this impertinence; this is no place for bagatelle; I have murdered my honour, destroyed a lady, and my desire of reparation is come at length too late. See there!

DURETTE
What ails her?

YOUNG MIRABEL
Alas, she's mad!

DURETTE
Mad! dost wonder at that? By this light, they're all so; they're cozening mad; they're brawling mad; they're proud mad: I just now came from a whole world of mad women, that had almost—What, is she dead?

YOUNG MIRABEL
Dead! Heavens forbid.

DURETTE

Heavens further it; for, till they be as cold as a key, there's no trusting them; you're never sure that a woman's in earnest, till she is nailed in her coffin. Shall I talk to her? Are you mad, mistress?

BISARRE

What's that to you, sir?

DURETTE

Oons, madam, are you there?

[Runs off.

YOUNG MIRABEL

Away, thou wild buffoon! How poor and mean this humour now appears? His follies and my own I here disclaim; this lady's phrensy has restored my senses, and, was she perfect now, as once she was, before you all I speak it, she should be mine; and, as she is, my tears and prayers shall wed her.

DUGARD

How happy had this declaration been some hours ago!

BISARRE

Sir, she beckons to you, and waves us to go off: come, come, let's leave them.

[Exeunt all but **YOUNG MIRABEL** and **ORIANA**.

ORIANA

Oh, sir!

YOUNG MIRABEL

Speak, my charming angel, if your dear senses have regained their order; speak, fair, and bless me with the news.

ORIANA

First, let me bless the cunning of my sex, that happy counterfeited phrensy that has restored to my poor labouring breast the dearest, best beloved of men.

YOUNG MIRABEL

Tune all, ye spheres, your instruments of joy, and carry round your spacious orbs the happy sound of Oriana's health; her soul, whose harmony was next to yours, is now in tune again; the counterfeiting fair has played the fool!

She was so mad, to counterfeit for me;
I was so mad, to pawn my liberty:
But now we both are well, and both are free.

ORIANA

How, sir? Free!

YOUNG MIRABEL

As air, my dear bedlamite! What, marry a lunatic! Lookye, my dear, you have counterfeited madness so very well this bout, that you'll be apt to play the fool all your life long.—Here, gentlemen!

ORIANA

Monster! you won't disgrace me!

YOUNG MIRABEL

O' my faith, but I will. Here, come in gentlemen.—A miracle! a miracle! the woman's dispossess'd! the devil's vanished!

Enter **OLD MIRABEL** and **DUGARD**.

OLD MIRABEL

Bless us! was she possessed?

YOUNG MIRABEL

With the worst of demons, sir! a marriage devil! a horrid devil! Mr. Dugard, don't be surprised. I promised my endeavours to cure your sister; no mad doctor in Christendom could have done it more effectually. Take her into your charge; and have a care she don't relapse. If she should, employ me not again, for I am no more infallible than others of the faculty; I do cure sometimes.

ORIANA

Your remedy, most barbarous man, will prove the greatest poison to my health; for, though my former phrensy was but counterfeit, I now shall run into a real madness.

[Exit; **OLD MIRABEL** after.

YOUNG MIRABEL

What a dangerous precipice have I 'scap'd! Was not I just now upon the brink of destruction?

Enter **DURETETE**.

Oh, my friend, let me run into thy bosom! no lark escaped from the devouring pounces of a hawk, quakes with more dismal apprehension.

DURETTE

The matter, man!

YOUNG MIRABEL

Marriage! hanging! I was just at the gallows foot, the running noose about my neck, and the cart wheeling from me.—Oh, I shan't be myself this month again!

DURETTE

Did not I tell you so? They are all alike, saints or devils!

YOUNG MIRABEL

Ay, ay: there's no living here with security; this house is so full of stratagem and design, that I must abroad again.

DURETTE
With all my heart; I'll bear thee company, my lad: I'll meet you at the play; and we'll set out for Italy to-morrow morning.

YOUNG MIRABEL
A match; I'll go pay my compliment of leave to my father presently.

DURETTE
I'm afraid he'll stop you.

YOUNG MIRABEL
What, pretend a command over me, after his settlement of a thousand pound a year upon me! No, no, he has passed away his authority with the conveyance; the will of the living father is chiefly obeyed for the sake of the dying one.

Dependence, ev'n a father's sway secures,
For, though the son rebels, the heir is yours.

[Exeunt severally.

ACT THE FIFTH

SCENE I.—The Street before the Playhouse

MIRABEL and **DURETETE**, as coming from the Play.

DURETTE
How d'ye like this play?

YOUNG MIRABEL
I liked the company;—the lady, the rich beauty, in the front box, had my attention: These impudent poets bring the ladies together to support them, and to kill every body else.

For deaths upon the stage, the ladies cry,
But ne'er mind us, that in the audience die:
The poet's hero should not move their pain,
But they should weep for those their eyes have slain.

DURETTE
Hoyty, toyty! did Phillis inspire you with all this?

YOUNG MIRABEL

Ten times more; the playhouse is the element of poetry, because the region of beauty; the ladies, methinks, have a more inspiring, triumphant air in the boxes than any where else—they sit, commanding on their thrones, with all their subject slaves about them;—Their best clothes, best looks, shining jewels, sparkling eyes; the treasure of the world in a ring.—I could wish that my whole life long, were the first night of a new play.

DURETTE
The fellow has quite forgot this journey;—have you bespoke post horses?

YOUNG MIRABEL
Grant me but three days, dear Captain, one to discover the lady, one to unfold myself, and one to make me happy, and then I'm yours to the world's end.

DURETTE
Hast thou the impudence to promise thyself a lady of her figure and quality in so short a time?

YOUNG MIRABEL
Yes, sir; I have a confident address, no disagreeable person, and five hundred Lewis d'ors in my pocket.

DURETTE
Five hundred Lewis d'ors! you an't mad!

YOUNG MIRABEL
I tell you, she's worth five thousand; one of her black, brilliant eyes, is worth a diamond as big as her head.

DURETTE
But you have owned to me, that, abating Oriana's pretensions to marriage, you loved her passionately; then how can you wander at this rate?

YOUNG MIRABEL
I longed for a partridge t'other day, off the king's plate, but d'ye think, because I could not have it, I must eat nothing?

Enter **ORIANA**, in Boy's Clothes, with a Letter.

ORIANA
Is your name Mirabel, sir?

YOUNG MIRABEL
Yes, sir.

ORIANA
A letter from your uncle, in Picardy.

[Gives the Letter.

YOUNG MIRABEL [Reads.]

The bearer is the son of a protestant gentleman, who, flying for his religion, left me the charge of this youth.—A pretty Boy!—He's fond of some handsome service, that may afford him opportunity of improvement: your care of him will oblige, Yours.
Hast a mind to travel, child?

ORIANA
'Tis my desire, sir; I should be pleased to serve a traveller in any capacity.

YOUNG MIRABEL
A hopeful inclination; you shall along with me into Italy, as my page.

DURETTE [Noise without.]
Too handsome—The play's done, and some of the ladies come this way.

[**LAMORCE** without, with her Train borne up by a **PAGE**.

YOUNG MIRABEL
Duretete, the very dear, identical she!

DURETTE
And what then?

YOUNG MIRABEL
Why, 'tis she!

DURETTE
And what then, sir?

YOUNG MIRABEL
Then!—Why, lookye, sirrah, the first piece of service I put upon you, is to follow that lady's coach, and bring me word where she lives. [To **ORIANA**.

ORIANA
I don't know the town, sir, and am afraid of losing myself.

YOUNG MIRABEL
Pshaw!

Enter **LAMORCE** and **PAGE**.

LAMORCE
Page, what's become of all my people?

PAGE
I can't tell, madam; I can see no sign of your ladyship's coach.

LAMORCE
That fellow has got into his old pranks, and fallen drunk somewhere;—none of the footmen there?

PAGE
Not one, madam.

LAMORCE
These servants are the plague of our lives—what shall I do?

YOUNG MIRABEL
By all my hopes, Fortune pimps for me! now, Duretete, for a piece of gallantry!

DURETTE
Why, you won't, sure?

YOUNG MIRABEL
Won't, brute!—Let not your servants' neglect, madam, put your ladyship to any inconvenience; for you can't be disappointed of an equipage, whilst mine waits below: and, would you honour the master so far, he would be proud to pay his attendance.

DURETTE
Ay, to be sure! [Aside.

LAMORCE
Sir, I won't presume to be troublesome, for my habitation is a great way off.

DURETTE
Very true, madam, and he's a little engaged; besides, madam—a hackney coach will do as well, madam.

YOUNG MIRABEL
Rude beast, be quiet! [To **DURETETE**.] The farther from home, madam, the more occasion you have for a guard—pray, madam—

LAMORCE
Lard, sir—

[He seems to press, she to decline it, in dumb show.

DURETTE
Ah! The devil's in his impudence! now he wheedles, she smiles—he flatters, she simpers—he swears, she believes—he's a rogue, and she's a w— in a moment.

YOUNG MIRABEL
Without there! my coach! Duretete, wish me joy!

[Hands the Lady out.

DURETTE
Wish you a—! Here, you little Picard, go follow your master, and he'll lead you—

ORIANA
Whither, sir?

DURETTE
To the Academy, child—'tis the fashion with men of quality, to teach their pages their exercises—go.

ORIANA
Won't you go with him too, sir? That woman may do him some harm, I don't like her.

DURETTE
Why, how now, Mr. Page, do you start up, to give laws of a sudden? Do you pretend to rise at court, and disapprove the pleasure of your betters?—Lookye, sirrah, if ever you would rise by a great man, be sure to be with him in his little actions; and, as a step to your advancement, follow your master immediately, and make it your hope, that he goes to a bagnio.

ORIANA
Heavens forbid!

[Exit.

DURETTE
Now would I sooner take a cart in company of the hangman, than a coach with that woman:—What a strange antipathy have I taken against these creatures! a woman to me, is aversion upon aversion! a cheese, a cat, a breast of mutton, the squalling of children, the grinding of knives, and the snuff of a candle.

SCENE II.—Lamorce's Lodgings

Enter **MIRABEL** and **LAMORCE**.

LAMORCE
To convince me, sir, that your service was something more than good breeding, please to lay out an hour of your company upon my desire, as you have already upon my necessity.

YOUNG MIRABEL
Your desire, madam, has only prevented my request:—My hours! Make them yours, madam, eleven, twelve, one, two, three, and all that belong to those happy minutes.

LAMORCE
But I must trouble you, sir, to dismiss your retinue, because an equipage at my door, at this time of night, will not be consistent with my reputation.

YOUNG MIRABEL
By all means, madam, all but one little boy—Here, page!

Enter **ORIANA**.

Order my coach and servants home, and do you stay; 'tis a foolish country-boy, that knows nothing but innocence.

LAMORCE
Innocence, sir! I should be sorry if you made any sinister constructions of my freedom.

YOUNG MIRABEL
O, madam, I must not pretend to remark upon any body's freedom, having so entirely forfeited my own.

LAMORCE
Well, sir, 'twere convenient towards our easy correspondence, that we entered into a free confidence of each other, by a mutual declaration of what we are, and what we think of one another.—Now, sir, what are you?

YOUNG MIRABEL
In three words, madam,—I am a gentleman, and have five hundred pounds in my pocket.

LAMORCE
And your name is—

YOUNG MIRABEL
Mustapha.—Now, madam, the inventory of your fortunes?

LAMORCE
My name is Lamorce—my birth, noble; I was married young, to a proud, rude, sullen, impetuous fellow;—the husband spoiled the gentleman;—crying ruined my face, till at last, I took heart, leaped out of a window, got away to my friends, sued my tyrant, and recovered my fortune.—I lived from fifteen to twenty, to please a husband; from twenty to forty, I'm resolved to please myself, and from thence, upwards, I'll humour the world.

YOUNG MIRABEL
Ha! ha! ha! I rejoice in your good fortune, with all my heart!

LAMORCE
O, now I think on't, Mr. Mustapha, you have got the finest ring there, I could scarcely believe it right; pray let me see it.

YOUNG MIRABEL
Hum! Yes, madam, 'tis—'tis right—but—but—but—but—but it was given me by my mother—an old family ring, madam—an old-fashioned, family ring.

LAMORCE
Ay, sir!—If you can entertain yourself for a moment, I'll wait on you immediately.

YOUNG MIRABEL
Certainly the stars have been in a strange, intriguing humour, when I was born.—Ay, this night should I have had a bride in my arms, and that I should like well enough! But what should I have to-morrow

night? The same. And what next night? The same. And what next night? The very same: Soup for breakfast, soup for dinner, soup for supper, and soup for breakfast again—But here's variety.

I love the fair, who freely gives her heart,
That's mine by ties of nature, not of art;
Who boldly owns whate'er her thoughts indite,
And is too modest for a hypocrite.

[LAMORCE appears at the Door; as he runs towards her, Four BRAVOES step in before her. He starts back.

She comes, she comes—Hum, hum—Bitch—Murdered, murdered, to be sure!
The cursed strumpet! To make me send away my servants—Nobody near me!
These cut-throats always make sure work.—What shall I do? I have but one way.
Are these gentlemen your relations, madam?

LAMORCE
Yes, sir.

YOUNG MIRABEL
Gentlemen, your most humble servant;—sir, your most faithful; yours, sir, with all my heart; your most obedient—come, gentlemen, [Salutes all round.] please to sit—no ceremony—next the lady, pray, sir.

LAMORCE
Well, sir, and how d'ye like my friends?

[They all sit.

YOUNG MIRABEL
O, madam, the most finished gentlemen! I was never more happy in good company in my life; I suppose, sir, you have travelled?

1ST BRAVOE
Yes, sir.

YOUNG MIRABEL
Which way, may I presume?

1ST BRAVOE
In a western barge, sir.

YOUNG MIRABEL
Ha! ha! ha! very pretty! facetious pretty gentleman!

LAMORCE
Ha! ha! ha! sir, you have got the prettiest ring upon your finger there—

YOUNG MIRABEL
Ah! Madam, 'tis at your service, with all my heart!

[Offering the Ring.

LAMORCE
By no means, sir, a family ring!

[Takes it.

YOUNG MIRABEL
No matter, madam.—Seven hundred pound, by this light! [Aside.

2ND BRAVOE
Pray, sir, what's o'clock?

YOUNG MIRABEL
Hum! Sir, I have left my watch at home.

2ND BRAVOE
I thought I saw the string of it, just now.

YOUNG MIRABEL
Ods my life, sir, I beg your pardon, here it is!—but it don't go.

[Putting it up.

LAMORCE
O dear sir, an English watch! Tompion's, I presume?

YOUNG MIRABEL
D'ye like, it, madam? No ceremony—'tis at your service, with all my heart and soul!—Tompion's! Hang ye! Aside.

1ST BRAVOE
But, sir, above all things, I admire the fashion and make, of your sword hilt!

YOUNG MIRABEL
I'm mighty glad you like it, sir!

1ST BRAVOE
Will you part with it, sir?

YOUNG MIRABEL
Sir, I won't sell it.

1ST BRAVOE
Not sell it, sir!

YOUNG MIRABEL
No, gentlemen, but I'll bestow it, with all my heart!

[Offering it.

1ST BRAVOE
O sir, we shall rob you!

YOUNG MIRABEL
That you do, I'll be sworn! [Aside.] I have another at home; pray, sir,—Gentlemen, you're too modest—have I any thing else that you fancy?—Sir, will you do me a favour? [To the First **BRAVO**.] I am extremely in love with that hat which you wear, will you do me the favour to change with me?

1ST BRAVOE
Lookye, sir, this is a family hat, and I would not part with it, but if you like it—

[They change Hats.]

—I want but a handsome pretence to quarrel with him—Some wine! Sir, your good health.

[Pulls **MIRABEL** by the Nose.

YOUNG MIRABEL
Oh, sir, your most humble servant! a pleasant frolic enough, to drink a man's health, and pull him by the nose! ha! ha! ha! The pleasantest, pretty-humoured gentleman—

LAMORCE
Help the gentleman to a glass.

[**MIRABEL** drinks.

1ST BRAVOE
How d'ye like the wine, sir?

YOUNG MIRABEL
Very good o'the kind, sir:—But I tell ye what, I find we're all inclined to be frolicsome, and 'egad, for my own part, I was never more disposed to be merry; let's make a night on't, ha!—This wine is pretty, but I have such burgundy at home! Lookye, gentlemen, let me send for half a dozen flasks of my burgundy, I defy France to match it;—'twill make us all life, all air, pray, gentlemen.

2ND BRAVOE
Eh? Shall us have his burgundy?

1ST BRAVOE
Yes, 'faith, we'll have all we can; here, call up the gentleman's servant.—

[Exit **FOOTMAN**.]

What think you, Lamorce?

LAMORCE
Yes, yes—Your servant is a foolish country boy, sir, he understands nothing but innocence.

YOUNG MIRABEL
Ay, ay, madam.—Here, Page,—

Enter **ORIANA**.

Take this key, and go to my butler, order him to send half a dozen flasks of the red burgundy, marked a thousand; and be sure you make haste, I long to entertain my friends here; my very good friends.

OMNES
Ah, dear sir!

1ST BRAVOE
Here, child, take a glass of wine—Your master and I have changed hats, honey, in a frolic.—Where had you this pretty boy, honest Mustapha?

ORIANA
Mustapha!

YOUNG MIRABEL
Out of Picardy—this is the first errand he has made for me, and if he does it right, I will encourage him.

ORIANA
The red burgundy, sir?

YOUNG MIRABEL
The red, marked a thousand, and be sure you make haste.

ORIANA
I shall, sir.

[Exit.

1ST BRAVOE
Sir, you were pleased to like my hat, have you any fancy for my coat?—Lookye, sir, it has served a great many honest gentlemen, very faithfully.

YOUNG MIRABEL
The insolence of these dogs is beyond their cruelty! [Aside.

LAMORCE
You're melancholy, sir.

YOUNG MIRABEL

Only concerned, madam, that I should have no servant here but this little boy—he'll make some confounded blunder, I'll lay my life on't; I would not be disappointed of my wine, for the universe.

LAMORCE

He'll do well enough, sir; but supper's ready; will you please to eat a bit, sir?

YOUNG MIRABEL

O, madam, I never had a better stomach in my life.

LAMORCE

Come, then, we have nothing but a plate of soup.

YOUNG MIRABEL

Ah! the marriage soup I could dispense with now. [Aside.—

[Exit, handing the **LADY**.

2ND BRAVOE

Shall we dispatch him?

3RD BRAVOE

To be sure; I think he knows me.

1ST BRAVOE

Ay, ay, dead men tell no tales; I han't the confidence to look a man in the face, after I have done him an injury, therefore we'll murder him.

[Exeunt.

SCENE III.—Old Mirabel's House

Enter **DURETETE**.

DURETTE

My friend has forsaken me, I have abandoned my mistress, my time lies heavy upon my hands, and my money burns in my pocket—But now I think on't, my myrmidons are upon duty to-night; I'll fairly stroll down to the guard, and nod away the night with my honest lieutenant, over a flask of wine, a story, and a pipe of tobacco.

[Going off, **BISARRE** meets him.

BISARRE

Who comes there? stand!

DURETTE

Heyday, now she's turned dragoon!

BISARRE
Lookye, sir, I'm told you intend to travel again.—I design to wait on you as far as Italy.

DURETTE
Then I'll travel into Wales.

BISARRE
Wales! What country's that?

DURETTE
The land of mountains, child; where you're never out of the way, 'cause there's no such thing as a highroad.

BISARRE
Rather, always in a high road, because you travel all upon hills; but be't as it will, I'll jog along with you.

DURETTE
But we intend to sail to the East Indies.

BISARRE
East, or West, 'tis all one to me; I'm tight and light, and the fitter for sailing.

DURETTE
But suppose we take through Germany, and drink hard?

BISARRE
Suppose I take through Germany and drink harder than you?

DURETTE
Suppose I go to a bawdy house?

BISARRE
Suppose I show you the way?

DURETTE
'Sdeath, woman! will you go to the guard with me, and smoke a pipe?

BISARRE
Allons donc!

DURETTE
The devil's in the woman!—Suppose I hang myself?

BISARRE
There I'll leave you.

DURETTE

And a happy riddance: the gallows is welcome.

BISARRE

Hold, hold, sir, [Catches him by the Arm, going.] one word before we part.

DURETTE

Let me go, madam,—or I shall think that you're a man, and, perhaps, may examine you.

BISARRE

Stir if you dare; I have still spirits to attend me, and can raise such a muster of fairies, as shall punish you to death.—Come, sir, stand there now, and ogle me: [He frowns upon her.] Now a languishing sigh: [He groans.] Now run, and take my fan,—faster.

[He runs, and takes it up.]

Now play with it handsomely.

DURETTE

Ay, ay.

[He tears it all in pieces.

BISARRE

Hold, hold, dear, humorous coxcomb! Captain, spare my fan, and I'll—Why, you rude, inhuman monster! don't you expect to pay for this?

DURETTE

Yes, madam, there's twelve pence; for that is the price on't.

BISARRE

Sir, it cost a guinea.

DURETTE

Well, madam, you shall have the sticks again.

[Throws them to her, and exit.

BISARRE

Ha! ha! ha! ridiculous, below my concern! I must follow him, however, to know if he can give me any news of Oriana.

[Exit.

SCENE IV.—Lamorce's Lodgings

Enter **YOUNG MIRABEL**.

YOUNG MIRABEL
Bloody hell-hounds! I overheard you:—Was not I two hours ago, the happy, gay, rejoicing Mirabel? How did I plume my hopes in a fair, coming prospect, of a long scene of years! Life courted me with all the charms of vigour, youth, and fortune; and to be torn away from all my promised joys, is more than death;—the manner too, by villains!—O my Oriana, this very moment might have blessed me in thy arms!—and my poor boy! the innocent boy! Confusion!—But hush, they come—I must dissemble still.—No news of my wine, gentlemen?

Enter the Four **BRAVOES**.

1ST BRAVOE
No, sir, I believe your country booby has lost himself, and we can wait no longer for't:—True, sir, you're a pleasant gentleman, but, I suppose you understand our business?

YOUNG MIRABEL
Sir, I may go near to guess at your employments; you, sir, are a lawyer, I presume—you a physician, you a scrivener, and you a stock jobber.—All cut-throats, egad! [Aside.

4TH BRAVOE
Sir, I am a broken officer; I was cashiered at the head of the army, for a coward, so I took up the trade of murder, to retrieve the reputation of my courage.

3RD BRAVOE
I am a soldier too, and would serve my king; but I don't like the quarrel, and I have more honour than to fight in a bad cause.

2ND BRAVOE
I was bred a gentleman, and have no estate; but I must have my whore and my bottle, through the prejudice of education.

1ST BRAVOE
I am a ruffian too; by the prejudice of education, I was born a butcher.—In short, sir, if your wine had come, we might have trifled a little longer.—Come, sir, which sword will you fall by? mine, sir?

2ND BRAVOE
Or mine?

[Draws.

3RD BRAVOE
Or mine?

[Draws.

4TH BRAVOE
Or mine?

[Draws.

YOUNG MIRABEL
I scorn to beg my life; but to be butchered thus!—O, there's the wine!—this moment for [Knocking.] my life or death.

Enter **ORIANA**.

Lost! for ever lost!—Where's the wine, child!

[Faintly.

ORIANA
Coming up, sir.

[Stamps.

Enter **DURETETE** with his Sword drawn, and six of the **GRAND MUSQUETEERS**, with their Pieces presented, the **RUFFIANS** drop their Swords.—**ORIANA** goes off.

YOUNG MIRABEL
The wine, the wine, the wine! Youth, pleasure, fortune, days and years, are now my own again! Ah, my dear friends! did not I tell you, this wine would make me merry?—Dear Captain, these gentlemen are the best natured, facetious, witty creatures, that ever you knew.

Enter **LAMORCE**.

LAMORCE
Is the wine come, sir?

YOUNG MIRABEL
O yes, madam, the wine is come—see there!

[Pointing to the **SOLDIERS**.]

Your ladyship has got a very fine ring upon your finger.

LAMORCE
Sir, 'tis at your service.

YOUNG MIRABEL
O ho! is it so? Thou dear seven hundred pound, thou'rt welcome home again, with all my heart!—Ad's my life, madam, you have got the finest built watch there! Tompion's, I presume?

LAMORCE
Sir, you may wear it.

YOUNG MIRABEL

O madam, by no means, 'tis too much—Rob you of all!—[Taking it from her.] Good, dear time, thou'rt a precious thing, I'm glad I have retrieved thee. [Putting it up.] What, my friends neglected all this while! Gentlemen, you'll pardon my complaisance to the lady.—How now! is it civil to be so out of humour at my entertainment, and I so pleased with yours? Captain, you're surprised at all this—but we're in our frolics, you must know.—Some wine here!

Enter **SERVANT**, with Wine.

Come, Captain, this worthy gentleman's health.

[Tweaks the First **BRAVO** by the Nose; he roars.

But now, where—where's my dear deliverer, my boy, my charming boy?

1ST BRAVOE

I hope some of our crew below stairs have dispatched him.

YOUNG MIRABEL

Villain, what say'st thou? dispatched! I'll have ye all tortured, racked, torn to pieces alive, if you have touched my boy.—Here, page! page! page!

[Runs out.

DURETTE

Here, gentlemen, be sure you secure those fellows.

1ST BRAVOE

Yes, sir, we know you, and your guard will be very civil to us.

DURETTE

Take them to justice.

[The **GUARDS** carry off the **BRAVOES**.]

Now for you, madam;—He! he! he! I'm so pleased to think that I shall be revenged of one woman, before I die.—Well, Mrs. Snap Dragon, which of these honourable gentlemen is so happy to call you wife?

1ST BRAVOE

Sir, she should have been mine to-night, 'cause Sampre, here, had her last night.—Sir, she's very true to us all four.

Enter **OLD MIRABEL, DUGARD**, and **BISARRE**.

OLD MIRABEL

Robin! Robin!—Where's Bob? where's my boy!—What, is this the lady? a pretty creature, 'faith!—Harkye, child, because my son was so civil as to oblige you with a coach, I'll treat you with a cart, indeed I will.

DUGARD
Ay, madam, and you shall have a swinging equipage, three or four thousand footmen at your heels, at least.

DURETTE
No less becomes her quality.

BISARRE
Faugh! the monster!

DURETTE
Monster! ay, you're all a little monstrous, let me tell you.

Enter **YOUNG MIRABEL.**

OLD MIRABEL
Ah, my dear Bob! art thou safe, man?

YOUNG MIRABEL
No, no, sir, I am ruined: the saver of my life is lost!

OLD MIRABEL
No, he came and brought us the news.

YOUNG MIRABEL
But where is he?

Enter **ORIANA.**

Ha!

[Runs and embraces her.]

My dear preserver! what shall I do to recompense your trust?—Father, friends, gentlemen, behold the youth, that has relieved me from the most ignominious death!—Command me, child; before you all—before my late, so kind, indulgent stars, I swear to grant whate'er you ask.

ORIANA
To the same stars, indulgent now to me, I will appeal, as to the justice of my claim: I shall demand but what was mine before—the just performance of your contract to Oriana.

[Discovering herself.

OMNES

Oriana!

ORIANA
In this disguise I resolved to follow you abroad, counterfeited that letter, that brought me into your service; and so, by this strange turn of fate, I became the instrument of your preservation; few common servants would have had such cunning; my love inspired me with the meaning of your message, because my concern for your safety made me suspect your company.

DURETTE
Mirabel, you're caught.

YOUNG MIRABEL
Caught! I scorn the thought of imposition—Caught! No, 'tis my voluntary act; this was no human stratagem, but by my providential stars, designed to show the dangers wandering youth incurs, by the pursuit of an unlawful love; to plunge me headlong in the snares of vice, and then to free me by the hands of virtue: Here, on my knees, I humbly beg my fair preserver's pardon; my thanks are needless, for myself I owe: And now, for ever, do protest me yours.

OLD MIRABEL
Tall, all di dall! [Sings.] Kiss me, daughter—no, you shall kiss me first, [To **LAMORCE**] for you're the cause on't. Well, Bisarre, what say you to the captain?

BISARRE
I like the beast well enough, but I don't understand his paces so well as to venture him in a strange road.

OLD MIRABEL
But marriage is so beaten a path, that you can't go wrong.

BISARRE
Ay, 'tis so beaten that the way is spoiled.

DURETTE
There is but one thing should make me thy husband—I could marry thee to-day, for the privilege of beating thee to-morrow.

OLD MIRABEL
Come, come, you may agree for all this;—Mr. Dugard, are not you pleased with this?

DUGARD
So pleased, that, if I thought it might secure your son's affection to my sister, I would double her fortune.

YOUNG MIRABEL
Fortune! has she not given me mine? my life—estate—my all? and what is more, her virtuous self?—Behold the foil [Pointing to **LAMORCE**.] that sets this brightness off! [To **ORIANA**.] Here view the pride, [To **ORIANA**.] and scandal of the sex!

What liberty can be so tempting there, [To **LAMORCE**.

As a soft, virtuous, am'rous bondage here?   [To **ORIANA**.

GEORGE FARQUHAR – A SHORT BIOGRAPHY

George Farquhar was born in Derry, Ireland in 1677, one of seven children born to William Farquhar, a clergyman. The author of "Memoirs of Mr. George Farquhar," a biographical sketch prefixed to certain 18th century editions of his works, claims that Farquhar "—discovered a Genius early devoted to the Muses. When he was very young, he gave Specimens of his Poetry; and discovered a Force of Thinking, and Turn of Expression, much beyond his Years."

Farquhar was educated at Foyle College and later, aged 17, he entered Trinity College, Dublin. Obviously rather young to be at university hence he entered as a sizar (an undergraduate who receives financial help from the college or, in this case, the Bishop of Dromore, and who has certain menial duties to perform in exchange for that support). Some accounts say that Farquhar may have initially intended to follow his father's profession and become a clergyman, but was, he seemed, unhappy and somewhat rebellious as a student and left Trinity after two years to become an actor.

There are several suggestions and accounts that Farquhar's early departure was down to his gay and volatile disposition and that he did not come to terms with "the Gravity and Retirement of a College-life." Yet another account argues that he was expelled from Trinity College due to a "profane jest."

With his education at an end a career had to be found. Farquhar joined a company performing on the Dublin stage, where he became an actor of no real talent at the Smock Alley Theatre in Dublin, probably through his acquaintance with the well-known actor Robert Wilks. Farquhar apparently had several failings as an actor; in no particular order we are informed that "his Voice was somewhat weak" and "his movements were stiff and ungraceful." Whilst his critics were many he was well received by audiences and this gave him the stamina to continue in this career "till something better should offer."

Some of the roles reportedly played by Farquhar were Lennox in Shakespeare's Macbeth, Young Bellair in The Man of Mode by George Etherege, Lord Dion in Philaster by Beaumont and Fletcher, and Guyomar in The Indian Emperor by John Dryden, a play in which his acting career would now come to an abrupt halt.

Whilst he was performing in the Dryden play, Farquhar's character was supposed to "kill" Vasquez, one of the Spanish generals in the drama. Unfortunately he failed to distinguish between a tipped foil and a deadly rapier, and seriously wounded a fellow actor named Price who was playing Valsquez. Although Price, in time, recovered, Farquhar resolved to give up acting for good.

Farquhar then left for London. Whether his actual intention was to begin writing, or to meet up with his friend, the noted actor Robert Wilks, who had received an offer from the manager of Drury Lane to come to London and join that theatre, and whether, in turn, Wilks had encouraged Farquhar to work harder on his writing and that London was the place to be in order to do that is only surmised.

His early plays were primarily spirited variations on a theme: young men have their fling for four acts and reform, usually unconvincingly, in the fifth. However, the plays from his talented pen have a freshness, however, as well as wit and human sympathy.

His first play, Love and a Bottle, was well received at London's Drury Lane Theatre in 1699 and was admired "for its sprightly Dialogue and busy Scenes," it is said to have been "well received by the Audience." Others called it a "licentious piece", and cited as proof that Farquhar had "absorbed the stock topics, character-types, and situations of Restoration comedy". The play deals with Roebuck, "An Irish Gentleman of a wild roving Temper" who is "newly come to London."

As the play opens Roebuck tells his friend Lovewell that he has left Ireland due to his getting a woman pregnant with twins (a boy and a girl) and because Roebuck's father was trying to force Roebuck to marry the woman; however, Roebuck remarks, "Heav'n was pleas'd to lessen my Affliction, by taking away the She-brat."

With the play a success Farquhar settled his talents on a career as a playwright. He had a second play open that same year; The Constant Couple. Again, it was warmly received on debuting at Drury Lane and proved a great success, helped considerably by his friend Wilks' portrayal of the character of Sir Henry Wildair, a performance that Farquhar himself praised generously in his "Preface to the Reader" when the play was published.

However, another interest and opportunity now unfolded into his life. He received a commission in the regiment of the Earl of Orrery. His time now became divided between the duties of a successful new playwright and the vocations of soldier.

That Farquhar was talented is indisputable but he also had an eye in promoting the talents of others. It was about this time that he discovered Anne Oldfield, who was reading aloud a scene from The Scornful Lady at her aunt's tavern. Impressed, he introduced her to Sir John Vanbrugh. This introduction led to the blossoming of her theatrical career, during which she was also the preferred performer of major female roles in Farquhar's later comedies.

In 1701 Farquhar wrote and debuted a sequel to the Constant Couple, called and based on its main character; Sir Harry Wildair.

The following year was to be prolific for the young playwright. He penned both The Inconstant or, The Way To Win (adapted from John Fletcher's Wild-Goose Chase) and The Twin-Rivals as well as publishing Love and Business, a collection that included letters, verse, and A Discourse Upon Comedy.

Interestingly the next year, he married Margaret Pemell, a widow with three children, ten years his senior, who it was said tricked him into marriage by pretending to have a great fortune. His biographer explains that "though he found himself deceived, his Circumstances embarrassed, and his Family increasing, he never upbraided her for the Cheat, but behaved to her with all the Delicacy and Tenderness of an indulgent Husband." However, this also misses the point that despite his success he was not earning a great deal financially from them and perhaps he was in search of a bride with the financial resources to enable him to live better than he did.

His work for the army, recruiting soldiers to fight in the War of the Spanish Succession, occupied much of his time for the next three years, and he was to write little except The Stage Coach, in 1774, a farce, in collaboration with Peter Motteux; that was adapted from a French play.

Farquhar was able, however, to draw upon these years of recruiting experience for his next comedy, The Recruiting Officer I, 1706.

Despite the success of his plays Farquhar had to sell his army commission to pay his debts, reportedly after the Duke of Ormond advised him to do so, promising him another but, it seems, failing to keep that promise.

Early in 1707, Farquhar's friend Wilks visited him; Farquhar was ill and in distress, and Wilks is said to have raised his spirits with a substantial present, and urged him to write another comedy. This comedy, was to be his masterpiece. The Beaux Stratagem, was given its première on March 8th, 1707. As can be easily gleaned from Farquhar's own statement prefacing the published version of the play he wrote it during his illness:

"The reader may find some faults in this play, which my illness prevented the amending of; but there is great amends made in the representation, which cannot be match'd, no more than the friendly and indefatigable care of Mr. Wilks, to whom I chiefly owe the success of the play."

In his last two plays his real contribution to the English drama is all the more apparent. He introduced a verbal vigour and sparring, as well as a love of character that are more usually associated with Elizabethan dramatists and laid much of the foundations for Sheridan and Congreve to build upon.

George Farquhar, aged only 40, died on April 29th, 1707, almost two months after the debut of his greatest work. He was buried in the Church of St. Martin in the Fields, London, on May 3rd, 1707.

GEORGE FARQUHAR – A CONCISE BIBLIOGRAPHY

Love and a Bottle, (1699)
The Constant Couple (1699)
Sir Harry Wildair (1701)
The Inconstant (1702)
The Twin Rivals (1702)
A Discourse Upon Comedy (1702)
The Stage Coach (1704)
The Recruiting Officer (1706)
The Beaux Stratagem (1707)

POEMS

THE ASSIGNATION

The Minute's past appointed by my Fair,
The Minute's fled
And leaves me dead
With Anguish and Despair.

My flatter'd Hopes their Flight did make
With the appointed Hour;
None can the Minute's past o'retake,
And nought my Hopes restore.

Cease your Plaints, and make no Moan,
Thou sad repining Swain;
Although the fleeting Hour be gone,
The Place doe's still remain.

The Place remains, and she may make
Amends for all your Pain;
Her Presence can past Time o'ertake,
Her Love your Hopes regain.

THE LOVERS NIGHT

The Nights black Curtain o're the World was spread,
And all Mankind lay Emblems of the Dead,
A deep and awful Silence void of Light,
With dusky Wings sat brooding o're the Night,
The rowling Orbs mov'd slow from East to West,
With Harmony that lull'd the World to rest.
The Moon withdrawn, the Oozy Flouds lay dead,
The very influence of the Moon was fled;
Some twinkling Stars, that thro' the Clouds did peep,
Seeming to wink as if they wanted Sleep,
All Nature hush'd, as when dissolv'd and lay'd
In silent Chaos e're the World was made;
Only the beating of the Lover's Breast
Made Noise enough to keep his Eyes from Rest;
His little World, not like the greater, lay
In loudest Tumults of disorder'd Day;
His Sun of Beauty shone, to light his Breast
With all its various Toils and Labours prest;
The Sea of Passions in his working Soul,
Rais'd by the Tempests of his Sighs did rowl
In towring Flouds, to overwhelm the whole,
Those Tyrants of the Mind, vain Hope and Fear,
That still by turns usurp an Empire there,
Now raising Man on high, then plunging in Despair.

Thus Damon lies, his Grief no Rest affords,
Till swelling full, it thus burst out in Words.
Oh! I could curse all Womankind, but one,
And yet my Griefs proceed from her alone.
Was not our Paradise by Woman lost?
But in this Woman still we find it most:
Hell's greatest Curse a Woman if unkind,
Yet Heaven's great Blessing, if she loves, we find.
Oh! if she lov'd, no God the Bliss cou'd tell,
She wou'd be Heaven it self, were she not so much Hell.
Thus our chief Joys with most Allays are curst,
And our best things, when once corrupted, worst.
But Heaven is just; our selves the Idols fram'd,
And are for such vain Worship justly damn'd.
Thus the poor Lover argued with his Fate;
Emilia's Charms now did his Love create;
That Love repuls'd, now prompted him to hate.
Sometimes his Arms wou'd cross his Bosom rest,
Hugging her lovely Image printed on his Breast,
Where flattering Painter Fancy shew'd his Art,
In charming Draughts, his Pencil Cupid's Dart.
The Shadow drawn so lively did appear,
As made him think the real Substance there.
Then was he blest, all Rapture, stunn'd with Joy,
Excess of Pleasure did his Bliss destroy;
He thought her naked, soft, and yielding waste
Within his pressing Arms lay folded fast;
Nay, by the Gods, she really there was plac'd;
Else how cou'd Pleasure to such Raptures flow?
Th' Effect was real—Then, the Cause was so.
What more can most substantial Pleasures boast
Than Joy when present, Memory when past?
Then, Bliss is real which the Fancy frames,
Or these call'd real Joys are only Dreams.

TO A GENTLEMAN, THAT HAD HIS POCKET PICKT OF A WATCH AND SOME GOLD BY A MISTRESS

I'm sorry, Sam, thour't such a Ninny
To Let a Wench rob thee of Guinea,
And thus to spend and lose your Cobbs,
By lavish opening both your Fobbs:
You're fairly fobb'd, to let her get all,
Both one, and also t'other Mettal.
Your Work was on a pretty Score,
You dug the Mine, she found the Oar;
The Devil take the cunning Whore.

You slily laid her down to rest her,
And on the Bed she found a Tester.
Your Watch too, Sam, (these Men of Power
Must lye with Doxies by the Hour)
A Minute's time did that command;
Then her's, it seems, was Minute Hand.
She wound you up to her own liking,
Then stole the Watch, while you were striking:
Then think not, Sir, that you are undone:
What's wound so high, must next be run down:
In revelling time you thought no Sin,
To play a Game, at In and In.
I wonder tho' you did not win for't,
Since that you were so fairly in for't:
But what destroy'd you in a Trice,
She held the Box, you shook the Dice:
The Devil was in the Dice then surely,
To loose when you plaid so securely,
And three to one was lay'd so purely.
But what's the worst of all Mishaps
You dread, they say, some After-claps:
If that be so, my dearest Sammy,
You'll curse, and bid the Devil dam ye:
The Fruit of Wild Oats which you scatter,
Is nothing else but Barley-Water:
The Seed-time's good, you know my meaning,
But Faith, the Harvest's only gleaning.
Take Heart howe're, 'tis my desire,
You will revive, the P—x expire;
Then rise like Phoenix from the Fire.
The Mettal's stronger that's well souder'd,
And Beef keeps sweeter once 'tis powder'd.
So farewell, Sam, and my you ne're want
Such a true faithful humble Servant.

www.ingramcontent.com/pod-product-compliance
Lightning Source LLC
Chambersburg PA
CBHW060143050426
42448CB00010B/2279